"Music is a reflection of our community and our community is a reflection of our music. The two are inseparable."

Ben Jaffe (Preservation Hall Jazz Band), p. 42

Contents

ON THE COVER

Every region in the US — in fact, everywhere in the world — has a long history of homegrown music. It would be impossible to calculate how many new styles of music have emerged from something that happened between a handful of musicians at somebody's house sometime. That's why we asked Asheville, North Carolina-based artist Colin Sutherland to create a front porch jam for our Homegrown theme. Look closely and you'll notice Levon Helm, Dave and Phil Alvin, Ben Jaffe, Candi Staton, and Kathleen Hanna are there. We'd like to be flies on the wall for *that* picking party.

Inside covers:
Illustrations by Drew Christie.

NO DEPRESSION TEAM
Chris Wadsworth *Publisher*
Kim Ruehl *Editor*
Stacy Chandler *Copy Editor/Social Media Manager*
Dave Champine *Operations*
Shelley Champine *Online Community Manager*
Sonja Nelson *Advertising*

WEB nodepression.com
TWITTER & INSTAGRAM @nodepression
FACEBOOK facebook.com/nodepression

GENERAL INQUIRIES
info@nodepression.com

ONLINE ADVERTISING
advertising@nodepression.com

SUBSCRIPTIONS
nodepression.com/subscribe

JOURNAL DESIGN & PRODUCTION
Brett Yasko
Printed in Canada by Hemlock Printers , 100% carbon neutral

No Depression is part of the FreshGrass Foundation.
freshgrass.org
ISBN: 978-0-9973317-2-1
©2016, FreshGrass, LLC

Hello Stranger

BY KIM RUEHL

Since I left home at the age of 19, there have been 19 apartments and houses across seven cities that I have, at one time or another, called home. Until I was in my 30s, I never really thought about what "home" means — the very concept seemed intangible and nonspecific. Because of my many moves, the entire continental United States felt like my neighborhood.

Even now, though I've lived in Asheville, North Carolina, for six years — in a house my wife and I own, where we're raising our child — I still occasionally wake in the morning thinking about that pho place on Broadway (in Seattle) where I'd like to go for lunch, or that particular hillside in Prospect Park (in Brooklyn) where I'd like to sit and read today. There's the good coffee shop down the street (in Portland) that knows my order, and the three-for-one happy hour with quarter oysters (in New Orleans) that I make a mental note to tell my wife we should really hit this afternoon ... until I remember it is literally hundreds of miles away. Nonetheless, these sort of muscle memory nostalgias make me grin. They've always tied the country together for me, made me feel at home almost anywhere I go.

But there's a difference between "feeling at home" and "home." Feeling at home is when your best friend's dog seems to recognize you even though months (or years) have passed. It's knowing where in your sister's cabinets you can find her secret candy stash.

But *home* is where your stuff lives — your instruments and books, your journals and desk. It's where your protective bubble is: where you sit and play the same four bars over and over for hours, existing, somehow, outside of time as you practice. It's where you record your friends in the basement, where you sit at your computer and design your album cover or flier or zine. Home is where your workshop is, where you house your collection of found objects that you plan to fashion into some kind of noisemaker.

Home is the town where you and your friends swap bandmates and sit in with one another, where you throw each other on the bill and promote each other's work. It's the town where you and the other musicians encounter noise ordinances and dancing bans, throw block parties and open mics and house shows for your friends from out of town. It's the porch you gather on to pick a tune.

Home, in other words, is where it all starts; it is where you build something from the ground up.

Home is where I am as I write this, surrounded by my toddler's toys and stacks of review copies of new albums. Where I have takeout boxes from my new favorite lunch spot (thankfully just three miles away), where my phone is plugged into the wall. It's where I can drink coffee from my favorite mug — the one given to me by the City of Nashville (where I've never lived), that reads, "Music is the reason I get up every afternoon." It's where this entire issue — like the last few issues of ND — has grown, from the ground up.

I have to admit, it's been particularly gratifying to see this one come together, as it is a sort of meeting place for so many of the times and places and scenes and styles and people that have made me personally feel at home over the past 19 years — Portland, New Orleans, Seattle, New York State. There's a lot of folk music in this issue, a lot of singer-songwriters. There are a lot of stories about the relationship between folk music and punk rock, the way those two musical worlds have punted a social conscience and worldview back and forth for decades. There are a lot of stories about the way families have impacted American roots music — from the Ardoins of Louisiana to the Whites of California, and on and on.

It was not my intention to make a book that is, in so many ways, so personal to me. But I reckon that's what happens when we start to talk about homegrown things.

Homegrown things have a way of holding a mirror to us — we see in them our own work and struggle, our own family and friends. I'm almost certain you, too, will see your own people and places in these stories. If even one of them can remind you of where you're most at home, then we've done our job.

NO DEPRESSION

L to R: Eric Gibson and Leigh Gibson.

PART OF A LINE

Why I love making music with my brother
by Leigh Gibson

"What we do now often seems like an extension of childhood. In a way, it's still our playtime."

Leigh Gibson

THIRTY YEARS AGO, WHEN MY brother Eric and I began our journey into the world of bluegrass music, we were the youngsters. The festival trail still had stalwarts Jim and Jesse, the Osborne Brothers, and the Whitstein Brothers entertaining audiences across the country. Now it seems we are the elder statesmen of brother duos. Though I find that fact hard to believe, I take that title with pride. I'm proud to be part of a brother duo. I share the same pleasure as other musicians: the opportunity to chase down sounds in my head and share them with an audience. But that pleasure is magnified because I'm doing it with a sibling.

People have long been drawn to the sound of siblings singing together. Examples of brothers and sisters singing together make up some of the earliest roots music recordings, beginning with the Carter Family and the Monroe Brothers. But I expect that long before any records were ever made, brothers and sisters came together to sing in their homes. Their music came about likely the same way ours did: in order to entertain ourselves, our family, and company in our home.

What makes sibling harmony so impressive and alluring? Some people think of it as something almost magical. I believe sibling groups share a few things that non-sibling singing groups do not. For one, acts like ours share the obvious genetic bond. Sibling voices sound similar to begin with. Much like two instruments built by a luthier from the same wood will sound similar, siblings have the benefit of learning to speak from the same people. The way a word is pronounced is something that can be traced from a country to a region to a locale, and can be even further filtered down into a family. In this way, I think a sibling act has an advantage. I say words and phrases the same way Eric does —and therefore we sing them alike — because we learned to do so from the same set of parents. My brother's singing tone matches mine and my sister's, and I hear it in my children as well.

Sibling acts also share an environment in which to develop as an act. There's no driving many miles to get together and rehearse. I only needed to look to the guy I shared a bedroom with growing up, who was only 11 months older than I, when I wanted to rehearse. We spent countless hours entertaining ourselves and our parents before we ever shared our music with the outside world. And what we do now often seems like an extension of childhood. In a way, it's still our playtime.

By the time we started singing together, we'd already created a short-hand of gestures and language that allowed us to understand, quickly and comfortably, what the other wanted or needed. I think that quickened our learning curve as a performing duo. We just added music to a partnership that already existed.

This kind of learned intuition helps set a sibling duo apart from other musicians. We are often able to anticipate what the other is going to do because of our bond. Often Eric will call out the very song I'm thinking of on stage, and will lead or follow an entirely new emotional delivery of a line with absolute confidence, because he somehow knows what I'm going to do.

Eric and I have always admired the Louvins and their album, *A Tribute to the Delmore Brothers*. When making our brother duet tribute, *Brotherhood*, which we released last year, we knew there were some acts we had to include. Groups like the Stanleys, Monroes, and Everlys were just too big to leave off the record. Other acts, like the Glaser Brothers, were so big in our house we had to include them. Otherwise, our only requirement for what songs we included on *Brotherhood* was: Did we feel like we were doing the other brother acts — and ourselves — justice by singing their song?

From making this record, we learned just how much the earlier acts borrowed or learned from one another. In early radio recordings of the Louvins, you can hear how much Ira affects his voice to sound like Bill Monroe, or how similar the Brewster Brothers' vocal style was to that of the Webster Brothers, who came from the same region in East Tennessee. Revelations like that taught us that we all come at this profession as fans of the music first, and that borrowing stylistic vocal ideas has always been a flattering tip of the cap from one brother act to another.

Now, looking behind us at the long line of music acts, I see many younger sibling groups coming along in bluegrass as well as other forms of roots music. Groups like the Zolla Boys, the Feinstein Brothers, the Quebe Sisters, and the Cactus Blossoms, to name a few, are developing their own style based on the long-practiced tradition of siblings singing together. I'm just happy and proud to be a part of that line. ■

BLOOD HARMONY

Sibling acts throughout history build on shared struggles and deep bonds

by Matt Powell

In a recurring Smothers Brothers bit, a frustrated Tom would yell out to brother Dick, "Mom liked you best!" It always got a laugh because it rang true. Stemming from the same seed, the sibling bond is unconditional, as adversarial as it is intuitive.

IRA LOUVIN HAD JUST LEFT A SOLO gig at the Chestnut Inn in Kansas City when a drunk driver struck his car head-on. His brother Charlie was on tour when he heard that his older brother had bled to death in the back seat of that car, along Highway 70, in an accident where whiskey and blood ran together. Charlie headed back to Nashville to arrange the funeral. But first, he finished his show.

Eight years later, another drunk driver, recently kicked out of a High Desert honky-tonk called the Jack of Diamonds, crashed into Clarence and Roland White as they loaded their equipment outside a gig at a Palmdale , California nightclub. Roland watched with a dislocated arm as his younger brother slipped into unconsciousness. Clarence died the next day.

In another time and place, for several minutes, Phil Alvin lay somewhere in the beyond. When Dave Alvin got the call that his older brother and former bandmate had died in Spain, he thought of all the music they hadn't made together. When Phil came back to this earthly realm, the estranged brothers cut a record and hit the road. "Life is too damn short," said Dave. "We gotta make up for lost time."

Sweet and Lovely, Hard and Mean

The dark rivers of American music run rich with blood. Blood in the wailing notes of the blues. Blood under a hot cotton sun, in the dark, coal-black air. The cleansing blood of salvation.

Music runs in the blood, too. Family bands have been a staple of American music since inception: from the Carter Family to the Staple Singers, the Beach Boys to the Ronettes, the Allmans to the Van Halens, the Isleys to the Jacksons. But there is an inimitable intimacy in pairs. Incubated in the Great Depression, brother and sister duos started picking together on whatever string instruments were around and harmonizing a cappella in the fields to pass the long days.

While circumstances of life have changed, that homespun collaborative urge remains for many. Phil and Dave Alvin did not grow up singing together. "We discovered music together much more than we played music together," remembers Dave. "We influenced each other by our shared passion."

The Alvins were roots music obsessives with an insatiable thirst, and the Los Angeles suburb of Downey proved unlikely fertile ground. "We had a lot of adventures searching for old 78s, 45s, and LPs, discovering obscure artists and sneaking into bars together to hear and experience the surviving masters," remembers Dave. "That music and those memories are a bond we share to this day."

Los Angeles in the 1970s was peppered with those surviving masters. Big Joe Turner and T-Bone Walker mentored the young Alvins. Sonny Terry gave Phil harmonica lessons. Saxophone great Lee Allen joined their band. The Blasters were a culmination of American roots music, from Tommy Duncan's yodel to Little Willie John's fevered shouts, fired back with punk abandon.

Phil's voice was a scream of authenticity tearing through the sounds of American music. When Dave started writing thoughtful songs, the brothers propelled each other, transcending imitation, even as the volatile nature of brotherhood wedged their eventual falling out.

"I think I didn't write enough songs in the old days that captured the glory of what Phil can do vocally," says Dave, "while I don't think he believed I could survive as a solo singer-songwriter/ guitar basher."

Through his acclaimed post-Blasters solo career, Dave Alvin has established himself as one of the finest songwriters of his generation. Like his journeyman blues mentors, Phil kept the Blasters going in various incarnations, to varying degrees of inspiration, seeming to hit a newfound stride leading up to his collapse.

It took Phil's flatlining in Spain to get them making music together as a duo. They went back to the well. *Common Ground* (2014), an album of Big Bill Broonzy covers, was neutral ground for the brothers to begin a new musical relationship. *Lost Time* followed in 2015, tapping into the same ferocious energy that sparked the Blasters. Dave sees this new pairing as a way to honor the living and dead, "to play some music not only for ourselves but all the old

musicians and teachers we had, our departed family members, and our long-gone friends."

The Alvin brothers are the last of a breed touched directly by original masters. Everything that came after them, no matter how good, is twice removed. Their reunion is both a homecoming and a journey forward — two estranged guardians, reunified, through whom the blood of American music flows.

Pictures from Life's Other Side

That blood spread in the 1920s, as people in the US began to move around, cross-pollinating ideas and experiences, connecting the rural poor through radio waves and internal combustion engines. Sibling harmony was born from shape-note singing, an abbreviated system of music notation easily learned without formal theory. The Sacred Harp hymnal, originally published in 1844, became the standard throughout the rural South. Only the Bible was found in as many homes.

Alton and Rabon Delmore's mother and uncle sang and composed gospel songs. Their father was a sharecropper. They toiled in the north Alabama cotton fields by day, and at night absorbed Southern gothic family lore. "The low lying hills always added a somber, sinister atmosphere to the tales of the people," Alton recalled in his posthumously published memoir, *Truth Is Stranger than Publicity.*

Alton taught younger brother Rabon the four-string tenor guitar and the two began meticulously working out their mellow, thoughtful harmonies. Alton studied guitar players like Jimmie Rodgers and Eddie Lang and adapted the sacred shape-note method his mother taught him to popular songs.

Another early duo, the Allen Brothers, advised Alton to write his own material. Alton took the advice to heart, penning over 1,200 songs, many of which became

standards. Columbia Records mistakenly placed the Allen Brothers' recordings, influenced by blues and riverboat jazz, in the "race" rather than "hillbilly" series. ("Hillbilly" music was treated with the same disdain as "race" music, even in the South.)

After World War II, the Delmore Brothers helped Syd Nathan launch King Records. Reuniting and reinventing themselves, they recorded a string of infectious boogie songs with the help of Henry Glover, an African-American piano player who worked mostly with King's R&B artists. These recordings, with their amplified guitars and driving beat, featured perhaps the earliest direct marriage of country music with R&B, foreshadowing rock and roll and rockabilly by almost a decade.

Personal tragedy and music business injustices caused the Delmore Brothers' collaboration to fall apart. Rabon split for Detroit and Alton shuffled through a variety of odd jobs. When he was diagnosed with lung cancer, Rabon sent for his brother. They played one final show and one final recording session together.

The Delmore Brothers made some of the most influential and exciting music to come out of the first half of the 20th century. They were the first superstar sibling duo. But they weren't alone.

Bill and Earl Bolick from Hickory, North Carolina, developed a soft singing style, with minimal guitar and mandolin accompaniment, to accentuate their clear harmonies. The Louvin Brothers and Everly Brothers later recorded songs like "Knoxville Girl" and "Kentucky" that they first learned from the Bolicks.

There were so many "brother duos" in the 1930s that the Bolicks billed themselves as the Blue Sky Boys, to avoid confusion, taking their name from the area of the Blue Ridge Mountains known as the "Land of the Sky."

The Bolick brothers returned from World War II to find a changing world with changing tastes. They refused

"We discovered music together much more than we played music together. We influenced each other by our shared passion."

Dave Alvin

to adapt to the post-war honky-tonk explosion or to add an electric guitar (a formula that brought the Louvin Brothers superstardom a decade later). Rather than compromise their home-spun sound, the Blue Sky Boys retired until the folk revival of the early-1960s provided a second act.

Other brother acts soared as well. The Dixon Brothers worked the Carolina textile mills and wrote and recorded popular songs including "I Didn't Hear Anybody Pray," about a car crash, immortalized by Roy Acuff as "Wreck on the Highway." The Callahan Brothers from Asheville, North Carolina, with their high-pitched yodels, were ARC's best-selling act. The Shelton Brothers cut almost 60 sides, including "Just Because," later covered by Elvis Presley. The York Brothers' hillbilly boogie shook the Motor City at a time when Southerners migrated north in droves to find manufacturing work.

Wiley and Zeke Morris taught themselves to play on a guitar older brother George won in a seed-selling contest. George learned to pick from a local musician who learned to play directly from Blind Lemon Jefferson on the streets of Johnson City. The two junior siblings formed the Morris Brothers.

Zeke once explained their strong, seamless harmonies: "We were brothers and had an advantage over most other groups. We always knew exactly what the other one was going to do." Riding high on Zeke's "Salty Dog Blues," they were offered an audition to replace the Delmore Brothers on the Opry, but Zeke refused to go to Nashville. The Wilburn Brothers got the slot.

However, it wasn't just brother groups that thrived around that time. Minnesota farm girls Mary Jane and Carolyn DeZurik "tried to sing with the birds," blending Scandinavian yodeling with the sounds of farm animals. They were immensely popular on shows like WLS's National Barn Dance, a significant Opry rival. The DeZuriks revived their act

following the war, making their Opry debut in 1944. Their new sponsor, the Purina Mills Company, changed their name to the Cackle Sisters. Though their repertoire comprised over 250 songs, the DeZurik Sisters recorded only six sides for the Vocalian label in 1938.

Teddy and Doyle Wilburn were children when they made their Opry debut in 1940. After the war, they became entrepreneurs who ran a publishing company and a booking agency and hosted their own television show for nine years, charting 30 hits from the 1950s to the 1970s. They cut "Knoxville Girl," which the Blue Sky Boys and Louvin Brothers had so memorably waxed. The narrator in "Knoxville Girl" bludgeons his girl with a stick, beating her merci-lessly as she begs for her life until the dirt is soaked in blood. He then throws her in the river before going home to mother.

That song was a hit for the Wilburn Brothers, but they turned down "Heartbreak Hotel," finding it "strange and almost morbid."

By the late 1960s, the Wilburns, who sang on street corners for coins during the Depression, were playing 250 dates a year. Teddy burned out, telling an interviewer in the late 1970s: "It was like a really bad country song, only I was actually living it, verse by verse."

When Doyle succumbed to cancer in 1982, Teddy described the loss of his brother and partner as feeling "like a 45-year marriage ended." He remained on the Opry until his death in 2003, the last of the duos reared in the Great Depression.

Depression-era sibling duos created a lasting and far-reaching influence in country music, most obviously in the many non-fraternal duos — Johnnie & Jack, Carl & Pearl Butler — and prominent duet pairings that continue to this day. More subtly, the reach of those early duos was felt in the two-part lead harmony that helped define the 1950s shuffles of Ray Price as well as the Bakersfield Sound of the 1960s.

Although hatched in Appalachia, sibling duos were not limited to Southern music. As children in the Bronx during the Depression, the daughters of Russian Jewish immigrants listened religiously to local Yiddish radio shows. After World War II, Clara and Minnie Bagelman became superstars of "Yiddish jazz" as the Barry Sisters, now Claire and Merna, with an impressive 40-year career. Claire called their perfect harmonies, which came forth with no formal training, "beshert" — a Yiddish word roughly translated as "meant to be."

One side effect of World War II was that Americans of varying ethnicities were introduced to each other for the first time. This co-mingling of subcultures shook up American demographics, launching a wealth of music. Santo and Johnny Farina's father was an Italian immigrant baker who discovered country music and, specifically, the steel guitar while stationed in Oklahoma. There were no steel guitars in the Farina brothers' Brooklyn neighborhood. The adults came from the old country. "All we heard was accordions and mandolins," Johnny once said in an interview. Their peers were all doing doo-wop.

As the Farina Brothers, they gained a following at school dances. One night after a gig they improvised a wistful steel guitar melody over doo-wop changes, played with the melodramatic vibrato inherent in Italian music. "Sleep Walk" became a number-one hit for Santo & Johnny in 1959 and remains a timeless treasure of instrumental music, bringing the steel guitar for the first time into rock and roll.

The Shadows of Undying Pain

Love and loss are the quintessential country music themes, but when siblings first joined in song they sang about what concerned them: God and murder.

"Ira was raised rougher," Charlie Louvin told Nicholas Dawidoff, author of *In the Country of Country: A Journey to the Roots of American Music.* "First one always gets more whippings."

Charlie and Ira Louvin (whose family name was Loudermilk) grew up hard. It was hard labor in the cotton fields around Sand Mountain, Alabama, where the Delmore Brothers were also raised. This Southern corner of Appalachia lies among the polar extremes of Saturday night sin and Sunday morning salvation. There was little nuance.

Their father was hard, sometimes walking six miles each way to work a 14-hour day for 50-cent wages. Yet he had strength left over to take the family to church every Sunday.

The boys learned music from his records — Blue Sky Boys, Monroe Brothers, Delmore Brothers — and singing from the Sacred Harp hymnal. Then one day Roy Acuff sped past the fields in an air-conditioned Franklin and everything clicked. Music was their way out. Their first paying gig earned them $4 — as much as their father made in eight days of hard labor.

Diminutive Charlie played guitar and sang lead while lanky Ira's fierce mandolin and high tenor belted with the passion and cadence of a Pentecostal preacher. Some of the Sand Mountain preachers handled snakes, but Ira had hellhounds on his trail, and that battle is in every note of his music. Some of their songs are mini-sermons, complete with Ira's spoken-word warnings against sin and its earthly and eternal consequences. Not exactly crossover material.

They never abandoned gospel music, but it was applying their shape-note harmonies and religious intensity to secular songs that brought the Louvin Brothers fame.

Raised among the brother duos they emulated and admired, they came to prominence in the 1950s — the era of the slick "Nashville sound" and rock and roll boogie. With their old-fashioned harmony and Ira's mandolin wrapped around a prominent electric guitar, the

Louvin Brothers created music that was eerily holy, ancient, and timeless.

Independently, Ira's high tenor was clearly discernable from Charlie's lower lead. But when blended together, even audiences watching in person could not always tell who was singing what. "In one line of a song we'd sometimes switch parts twice," recalled Charlie. All of a sudden, Ira would swoop down while Charlie went high, seemingly without cue. "We did it instinctively," Charlie said. Brothers have that advantage.

And brothers can be cursed.

Ira Louvin fell to show business temptation, and his demons proved too strong to sustain. He began a tortured cycle of drinking followed by guilt, assuaged by more drinking and violence. He smashed his mandolin on more than one stage, when he showed up at all.

In 1961, when he tried to strangle his wife with a telephone cord, she unloaded a .22 pistol into him. "If the son of a bitch don't die, I'll shoot him again," she told police. Ira didn't die that night. After the split with Charlie two years later, Ira planned to buy a tent and preach the gospel after one last string of solo shows. He never made it off the lost highway.

Ira's intensity was both a detriment to and part of the brothers' veritable and seductive sound. "He'd sing so high the veins would pop out on his forehead," Chet Atkins once said. This intensity ignited his fervent musical sermons. But he also wrote songs of aching beauty, like "When I Stop Dreaming," sung with those swirling fraternal harmonies until they became a tender, singular voice.

In the early 2000s, Charlie opened a small storefront museum in Nashville near the Opry, where he continued to play until he was overcome by cancer. Visitors could peruse the glass cases of belt buckles, pocket knives, and other souvenirs from his life. On the wall hung framed black-and-white photographs of his brother's wreck on the highway.

The Louvin Brothers remain the gold standard of Appalachian sibling

harmony. But two brothers from Kentucky created a sound that resonated across the pond and the universe in cumulate echoes.

What Would Life Be?

Don and Phil Everly grew up in the family band. Their father, Ike, was influenced by African-American guitar players he heard as a kid in Muhlenberg County, Kentucky, and his distinctive finger-picking directly influenced Merle Travis, who directly influenced Chet Atkins and Scotty Moore, whose rudimentary fingerpicking helped invent rock and roll guitar.

They were country from the start, raised on the Blue Sky Boys and Delmore Brothers. Don's personal favorites were Hank Williams, Lefty Frizzell, and the haunting group harmony of the Sons of the Pioneers, before turning to Ray Charles, Sonny Terry and Brownie McGhee, and the exotic tunings and hypnotic rhythms of Bo Diddley.

The Everly Brothers were victims of their circumstance. They were true artists trapped within music business confines. Their publisher, Wesley Rose, was also their manager. This insurmountable conflict of interest prevented the brothers from recording songs Rose didn't own. But the brothers fought for their art. They essentially produced their own records, uncredited, adding distinctive, Diddley-esque guitar intros to songs like "Bye, Bye Love" and "Wake Up Little Susie," making otherwise unexceptional novelty timeless.

Don suggested "Let It Be Me," which they had to fight Rose to record, after hearing an instrumental version by Chet Atkins. Don asked if there was a lyric. Chet said, "Yes, and it's a great one."

Always looking to explore new musical ground, their management and label kept throwing them well-crafted, but adolescent, novelty: "Poor Jenny," "Bird Dog," "Problems."

In 1958, Don and Phil walked into a Nashville studio with only their guitars, upright bass player Lightnin' Chance, and the dark echo of the Kentucky hills. The resulting *Songs Our Daddy Taught Us*, a collection of traditional ballads they had sung all their life, was a statement, establishing their rightful place in the line from the Blue Sky Boys and Delmore Brothers through the Louvins and into the rock era.

Timing is everything, and the Everlys were always either one step ahead or left behind. The bulk of their brilliant 1960s output was ignored by American audiences, who associated them with malt shop nostalgia. Arriving in England, they were told they sounded like the Beatles. They didn't know what that meant.

The Everlys' influence is infinite. It's in John Lennon and Paul McCartney's two-part leads — it was their whole sound. The Beatles, like Elvis, were a prism through which their influences filtered, indirectly affecting music the world over for generations.

The Everly Brothers brought Depression-era sibling harmony into the modern mainstream. Then they invented the template for British Invasion rock. In 1968 they released *Roots*, foreshadowing country-rock. This was cemented with 1972's *Pass the Chicken & Listen* and *Stories We Could Tell*, featuring Clarence White on guitar. Artists like Gram Parsons and the Byrds rode the glory of this new sound, while the brothers who helped originate it were reduced to the amusement park circuit.

On July 14, 1973, Phil smashed his guitar on stage at Knott's Berry Farm, vowing never to play with his brother again. A drunken Don finished the show alone, assuring the audience, "the Everly Brothers died 10 years ago."

They didn't speak until a redemptive 1983 reunion. They were great, but it was the hits for the old folks. They never found the urge for one last musical statement, one great September album. Phil died in 2014. The Kentucky son, whose coal-mining father fell to black lung, smoked himself to death.

The tragedy of the Everly Brothers is in the trappings of circumstance and in the brothers themselves. The chemistry that sparks such glorious music is combustible. Recurring themes — drugs and disappointment, ego and pride — built walls the brothers never surmounted. But when they joined voices in song, it was the apex of ancient and modern worlds.

Sweet Suburban Songs

As sibling duos sprouted across Appalachia during the Depression, dustbowl migrants flocked to the Promised Land of California, seeking work in the agricultural Central Valley. With World War II came an explosion of manufacturing jobs in the boomtown of Los Angeles. Country music was king in blue-collar suburbs stretching from Long Beach up through the South Gate to the city. Hillbilly variety shows like Town Hall Party in Compton dominated the radio airwaves and local television.

The influx of Southern migrants, the proximity of the film and recording industries, the agricultural and equestrian topography, and plentiful factory work culminated in a rich country and western culture. Los Angeles of the 1950s was hillbilly heaven.

Raised in a large musical family on an Oklahoma dairy farm, Lorrie and Larry Collins were 11 and 9 years old when they first appeared on Town Hall Party in 1954, taking the local scene by storm.

Lorrie was a rock and roll and rockabilly pioneer. She dated Ricky Nelson briefly, appearing as his steady on his family show, *The Adventures of Ozzie and Harriet*. Larry was mentored by guitar ace Joe Maphis, beating out his fiery rhythm with abandon on a custom Mosrite double neck. When they teamed up as the Collins Kids, it was pure, as host Tex Ritter said, "T double-N T!"

The Collins' youthful charm and genuine mutual admiration made for a crowd-pleasing five-year run of electric performances and local hit records like "Hot Rod," which they performed decked out in custom suits by tailor Nudie of Hollywood, straight outta Compton.

The Collins Kids had a mutual burnout more than a falling out. They agreed from the start to hang it up as soon as it stopped being fun. Lorrie got engaged, then pregnant, and eased gracefully into family life. Larry went on to write "Delta Dawn" for Tanya Tucker and "You're the Reason God Made Oklahoma" for Lefty's brother, David Frizzell.

Revivalists in the 1990s coaxed the Collins Kids back into the worldwide rockabilly festival circuit. Though they never achieved true national success, in the matters that count, they remain a sibling success story.

Growing up north of Los Angeles, Clarence and Roland White saw Joe Maphis and Merle Travis perform live at Town Hall Party. The guitarists mentored the young brothers as they started making a name for themselves around town as brilliant bluegrass pickers.

With his uncanny sense of time and phrasing and lightning-quick runs, Clarence White singlehandedly revolutionized the guitar twice: first as an acoustic lead instrument in bluegrass, a genre notoriously resistant to change, and later with Telecaster electricity, helping to create what became country-rock. Roland remains one of the great mandolin and guitar players in traditional and progressive bluegrass.

The brothers formed the Kentucky Colonels before venturing into equally impressive solo careers. Clarence found ample session work backing up artists including West Coast country-rock pioneers the Gosdin Brothers (Vern Gosdin went on to make some of the finest country records of the 1980s), Wynn Stewart, Joe Cocker, Randy Newman, and the Everly Brothers. He also joined the Byrds for five years.

Roland, meanwhile, went back to his roots, switching to guitar to play in the bands of his heroes, Lester Flatt and Bill Monroe — a gig for which Roland was recommended by his younger brother Clarence.

Before Clarence was killed, the brothers reunited, arriving from different musical ends to the same sweet place. With the Byrds, Clarence essentially created a subgenre, B-bending his brand of country guitar into the stratosphere. Roland was coming off six years' tutelage in the bands of the original bluegrass masters, digging deeper in the soil. Roland once described their brief reunion as the White Brothers as "the best time I had playing music — ever."

After dinner at their mother's house in Lancaster one night in 1973, they headed to a local club to sit in with brother Eric's country band. It was in the parking lot after that gig that a drunk driver plowed into the White Brothers. It was earlier that same night, 90 miles away, when Phil Everly smashed his guitar on stage, ending the Everly Brothers.

Less than a decade earlier, in the nearby suburb of Downey, the fresh-faced, light jazz Richard Carpenter Trio began featuring its namesake's younger sister, Karen, on drums. Eventually, Karen started singing pop numbers, still behind her kit, and Richard arranged lush vocal harmonies inspired by the Beach Boys from nearby Hawthorne.

Whatever one may think of Richard Carpenter's taste, he was obviously gifted. He was a simultaneous musical square and visionary. "We've Only Just Begun," for example, started as a bank commercial. Everyone laughed, until it sold a million copies.

Karen was ahead of her time as a female drummer, but it was the pain in her undeniable voice that transcended any distracting production values.

The Carpenters' story is frustrating and tragic, and the dynamic between the siblings is complicated and often misunderstood. Postwar suburban Los Angeles was a far cry from Depression-era Appalachia, yet the impulse that brought duos like the Delmores together was the same that brought the Carpenters together, musically. It is easy to opine that Karen might have made better music independently, but they brought out the best in each other in their way.

Richard coaxed Karen out from behind her security blanket to sing center stage. This rattled her already fragile self-esteem. She referred to being onstage, feeling naked and vulnerable, as having "to go face the wolves again." But Richard was responsible for getting those perfect performances out of his sister. Whether he fostered her sadness, or provided her a mechanism to express it, remains up for debate.

The emotional and physical exhaustion of superstardom and relentless touring compounded Karen's already delicate condition. Richard got hooked on Quaaludes while Karen wasted away from anorexia nervosa, withering into literal skin and bones until she collapsed at her parents' home from a poisoned and weakened heart. She was 32.

Back A Little Further

"Monroe Brothers was great, but Bill Monroe and his Blue Grass Boys are greater," Bill Monroe told Jim Rooney, author of *Bossmen: Bill Monroe and Muddy Waters.*

The Monroe Brothers got their start during the Depression, but quickly set themselves apart from the competition by playing with a faster dexterity and singing with a higher intensity. Bill almost single-handedly popularized the mandolin. While other acts, like the Blue Sky Boys, were playing intentionally restrained accompaniment to their quiet vocal harmony, Bill Monroe quickly proved himself a master of his instrument.

Bill, Charlie, and Birch Monroe were as stubborn as brothers can be. "So many times brothers can't get along good, you know," Bill recounted, "One wants to be the boss and the other one's mad because he does and so it was just better that we split up." Charlie once said simply, "We were hot-headed and mean as snakes."

Charlie Monroe formed his own band and recorded well into the 1950s. When introspective, younger Bill formed the Blue Grass Boys — igniting a firestorm and inventing a new genre — he did it without his brother. Nonetheless, other sibling duos, like the Stanley Brothers, Osborne Brothers, and Jim & Jesse, pushed boundaries within Monroe's new genre, often spilling over into mainstream country and attracting collegiate folk audiences.

Ralph Stanley's mournful, primordial tenor wailed around brother Carter's warm and resonant leads like a bat in a belfry. "I was singing music long before bluegrass," he told Nicholas Dawidoff, for *In the Country of Country.*

The Stanley Brothers sang Appalachian songs, hymns, and the sibling duo staple: the murder ballad. "When they have disputes and arguments," Ralph said of his poor and violent upbringing in southwest Virginia, "it often leads to a killin'. It's that way everywhere. In the cities you heard about it through newspapers. Here, back in the country, you heard about it through songs."

Carter was the leader and a prolific songwriter. He drank himself to death in 1966, when he was 41, reduced to a footnote in the long shadow of his baby brother's continued success as an ambassador of a near-ancient musical tradition.

Siblings break up — they die, they quit, they go solo. The survivor carries on in different ways. Some, like Alton Delmore, quietly retire. Some, like Bill Monroe, push their music to even greater heights. Ralph Stanley dug deeper into the roots of his Appalachian balladry, immersing himself in American song

"Their response time with each other is instantaneous, and they sing so perfectly every time, it's difficult to pick a take. To watch those girls work is to witness a magic trick."

Tim Hanseroth on the Secret Sisters

L to R: Phil Hanseroth, Brandi Carlile,
Tim Hanseroth

old as its blood-dimmed soil: "I'd say, if anything after Carter passed away, I took it back a little further."

All of These Lines

The sibling song plays on. Duos like Matthew & Jill Barber, the Avett Brothers, and the Cactus Blossoms are making new and exciting music from fraternal foundations. The Avetts — Scott and Seth — have fused bluegrass and stringband sounds with pop hooks and punk energy, garnering critical and commercial success. At the center of it all is that inimitable sibling sound.

"Both Scott and Seth are great lead and harmony singers," says Tim Hanseroth. "When you see them play you just want to sing the third part all night. They know how to put you in the song with them."

Tim and his twin brother, Phil Hanseroth, known as "the Twins," played around their native Seattle before teaming up with Brandi Carlile in the early 2000s. When Phil married Carlile's sister, they effectively became a family band, something evident in their process and music.

"We find our harmonies naturally," says Phil of working with Tim. "We don't think about it — it just happens." The twin dynamic makes for instinctive but cautious choices. "As twins we have to be thoughtful to not get complacent," Tim says. Then, as if finishing his brother's thought, Phil adds, "We try not to approach new songs the same way twice. We never want to have a formula."

Like the duos of the Depression, the twins come from a musical family. Their father taught them chords on an old nylon string guitar he picked up in the Navy. "We always played together, making up songs. Our dad is still showing me chords and riffs," says Phil.

The twins were drawn early to oldies radio and their parents' records, including Simon & Garfunkel, the Four Seasons, and the otherworldly sibling harmonies of the Beach Boys. Punk bands like the Dead Kennedys made playing music seem accessible.

The twins' Grammy-nominated work with Carlile proves family bands — and

"As twins we have to be thoughtful to not get complacent."

Tim Hanseroth

sibling pairings specifically — translate artistically and commercially into the modern age.

These days, along with Carlile, the twins are producing an album for another sibling group: the Secret Sisters.

The Secret Sisters' sound is steeped in their Alabama roots. Lydia and Laura Rogers, from the fertile Tennessee River soil of Muscle Shoals, started singing together in a church without instruments, about the closest you can find to shape-note in modern times.

Like their heroes the Everly Brothers, Lydia and Laura are no strangers to show business victories and losses. The sisters' familial harmonies and grounded writing have put them on stages opening for Nickel Creek, Elvis Costello, and Willie Nelson, and in studios with Jack White and T Bone Burnett. They wrote a song by proxy with Bob Dylan. They even penned a modern-day murder ballad, "Iuka," bringing the sibling duo phenomenon full circle.

Dropped by their label and sued by their former manager, Laura resorted to cleaning houses to make ends meet. She and her sister depend on each other for the same support as Depression-era duos. Instead of calling it quits, together they dug in. Crowdsourcing their third album so they could make it themselves, they explained, "We slowly crafted a batch of songs that were the result of one question: What are you left with when you've lost everything?"

One answer is family. Lydia and Laura's father, a local bluegrass musician, exposed the sisters to a wealth of music early on: from shape notes at the Church of Christ to George Jones records on Sunday mornings to the non-fraternal harmonies of the Four Seasons cassette in his truck. The sisters made music individually for years before joining

together. But when they did, they arrived with the same instincts.

"Their response time with each other is instantaneous, and they sing so perfectly every time, it's difficult to pick a take," says Tim Hanseroth, "To watch those girls work is to witness a magic trick."

Lost Time

Sibling music spans genre, geography, and time. Although not exclusively an American phenomenon — Canadian twins Tegan and Sara, Swedish sisters First Aid Kit, and British electronic duo Disclosure come to mind — the kernel bred in Appalachia spread across America and continues into the 21st century.

In a recurring Smothers Brothers bit, a frustrated Tom would yell out to brother Dick, "Mom liked you best!" It always got a laugh because it rang true. Stemming from the same seed, the sibling bond is unconditional, as adversarial as it is intuitive.

"We're not competitive with music or anything else," says Phil Hanseroth, speaking on how the twins have managed to avoid sibling ego pitfalls. "We came up sharing everything and got to where we are against odds," adds his brother. "We're grateful to do what we do whether we're sharing victories or losses."

For Dave and Phil Alvin, the competitiveness that sparked so much musical intensity and personal friction earlier in their lives has given way to respect. The passion that brought them together musically kept them apart for years. Now it has come full circle, allowing the brothers that rare and unpromised second chance.

The Alvins grew up in the same city as Richard and Karen Carpenter, but a

world apart. In "Downey Girl," his 2009 tribute to Karen, Dave Alvin examines the refined empathy that comes with the maturity and mellowing of age — the same perspective that would eventually reopen doors with his brother.

"We respect and appreciate each other more now," says Dave, "This newly found respect and appreciation makes the music we play now feel a lot like the early days."

The strange brew of blood harmony is potent. It binds and it destroys. Its stains do not wash out. Decades after their split, Charlie Louvin still moved to the side of the microphone during a Louvin Brothers song when it came time for Ira's high tenor part. Richard Carpenter told his sister he loved her before she died, but he hasn't gotten over the loss. In the 2002 BBC documentary *Close to You: The Story of the Carpenters*, he said, "You do think about ... how much more music was in the two of us." Likewise, Don Everly confessed in a *Los Angeles Times* interview a few months after Phil's death: "I always assumed I would go first, because I was the oldest. I'm not over it."

And now, in a studio outside of Seattle, the Secret Sisters and the Hanseroth twins are recording new songs of pain and redemption. On a stage somewhere across America or the world, Dave and Phil Alvin are plugging in, ready to strike an older, wiser chord, but just as loud — born from brotherly love, voiced from newfound respect, bound by a bloodline no rank strangers could emulate.

The ancient sounds of sibling blood will continue for all time. Time not lost so much as suspended somewhere in the space between brother and sister joining together in song, as inevitable an urge as drawing breath. ∎

DAVID McCLISTER

L to R: Page Burkum and Jack Torrey.

BAND OF BROTHERS

**The Cactus Blossoms
dream up a future that
pulls from the past**

by Stacy Chandler

THE WORLD IS FULL OF SONGS extolling one's object of affection as something superlative: the brightest star in the sky, the sweetest-smelling rose in the garden. Royalty is a common theme, too, and it appears in the Cactus Blossoms' song "Queen of Them All," but that's where expectations are overthrown: Among other praise, the fair lady is lauded with the swoon-worthy line, "you're my best-fitting pair of jeans."

It's easy to want to shove the Cactus Blossoms — brothers Jack Torrey and Page Burkum, from Minneapolis, Minnesota — into accessible categories like brother harmony and retro rock. It's impossible to hear them and not think of the Everly Brothers. But just when you think you've got them pinned down, something shifts.

They don't *look* like a retro act, for one thing. They favor jeans and casual shirts onstage, displaying nary a whiff of pinstripe or letter jackets. And while they may tend toward vintage guitars, Torrey insists it's more a matter of thrift than tradition. They listened to some Everly Brothers growing up, but only in between the standard mainstream music typical of many children of the 1980s.

Perhaps the only stereotype that really works for this duo is the age-old story of siblings who dipped their toes into music — first separately, later together. As a duo, they eventually scored a Monday night gig at a local club, then finally landed a big break.

Comes Naturally

You're Dreaming (released Jan. 22 on Red House Records) is 11 songs of close harmonies that include "Stoplight Kisses" — a playful ode to the lost art of car makeouts — and laments stewed from good old-fashioned heartbreak. But there's also more edgy fare addressing obsessive flights of jealousy and downward spirals that may lead to a "dive off River Street."

Many of the songs were honed over a year and a half of a practice-in-public gig at Turf Club in nearby St. Paul. They emerged to augment long set lists of covers that included lots of classic country music by folks like Ray Price, the Louvin Brothers, and the Delmore Brothers. A fellow musician friend familiar with their sound would toss out a song idea, and the brothers would give it a try.

"We didn't practice," Torrey says. "We just kind of threw in songs and tried them out. Whichever ones felt okay, we'd try again, and then improve on [them] a little bit."

Their sound — infused with echoes of the past but cut from a more modern cloth — emerged in a similarly organic way. "Maybe a little bit of it came naturally," Torrey conjectures, "and I think the rest is just a lot of time spent together."

About five years apart in age, Torrey (the youngest) and Burkum (the middle kid — their older brother Tyler Burkum played electric guitar on "You're Dreaming" and sometimes joins them on tour) don't display any sibling rivalry onstage. Their voices blend so closely, it's sometimes hard to pick out who's singing lead and who's holding down the harmony.

"Every set of brothers out there yell at each other and fight a little bit as kids, but that was more of just a kid thing for us," says Burkum. "We've gotten along pretty well since we were old enough to really hurt each other."

Growing up, the brothers mainly listened to what their parents had in their collection, which was heavily stocked in the '70s. "I think we had a lot of stuff around that most people had," says Burkum, recalling plenty of Stevie Wonder but also Paul Simon's *Graceland* and music from the Beatles and the Everly Brothers. When they got older, "we all got into bands like everybody does in high school," he adds. "For me and Tyler, it was the grunge era, but we would listen to a little bit of everything." Everything, that is, except folk and country music. "That wasn't really a big thing in our house."

But years later, after Torrey started playing electric bass and Burkum learned his way around a drum set, some country and folk sounds started seeping in. Playing separately with friends and alone, Burkum was learning Jimmie Rodgers songs, "and I learned about as many Dylan songs as my brain could hold at once," Torrey says. He found, however, that he wasn't having much fun playing on his own. "Me and Page started singing together, and there were like two songs we realized we could sing together on. So that's how we started."

Among those early songs were the Delmore Brothers' "Blue Railroad Train," Mississippi Sheiks' "Blood in My Eyes," and Ray Price's "Crazy Arms" — "whatever we could find that worked well with harmony," Burkum says.

Burkum, who'd also been learning guitar, found he had a knack for picking out harmonies, and the path became clear. "Jack and I started playing together and I ditched the drum set," he says.

Northern Isolation

If you don't know much about Minneapolis, you know at least two things: It gets cold there. And despite that — or maybe because of it — it's a hotbed for all kinds of music. The Twin Cities (St. Paul is just across the Mississippi River) provided fertile ground for Prince, the Replacements, the Jayhawks, Soul Asylum, Babes in Toyland, Hüsker Dü, and more.

"It is a supportive place," says Torrey, half-jokingly chalking it up to "Northern isolation. Cold, lonely winters." The tight-knit music community means a band like the Cactus Blossoms can end up on all sorts of bills; the music doesn't necessarily need to match, he says. "It all comes together and ends up being a great night. It's a really cool city that way."

It has geography going for it, too, Burkum adds. "It's not really on the way to anywhere. ... I think in a weird way that has allowed some space for Minneapolis bands to have their own scene. Our venues aren't always flooded by a million bands passing through." He adds with a laugh: "We have to entertain ourselves."

It was in Minneapolis that Torrey and Burkum first met Nashville-by-way-of-Oklahoma singer-songwriter JD McPherson, when they opened for him at the storied club First Avenue. When the brothers — then doing mostly country and western covers backed by fiddle and pedal steel — started their set, McPherson had busied himself backstage. But when they launched into an original ("Adios Maria," which

"When we hear something back, we're like, 'God, why does that sound kind of old? I was born in 1986, what's going on here?' I think it's just something that comes naturally to us."

Jack Torrey

appears on *You're Dreaming*), "I was kind of just drawn out to the main floor," McPherson recalls. "I listened to it really carefully." Then and there, he called his manager, who had put the show together, and told him, "Man, there's something special about these guys."

He started bumping into the brothers at other shows and festivals, and before long, McPherson asked how many new songs they had, and whether they were thinking of recording an album. "He just said, 'I want to help out as much as I can,'" says Torrey. It was an offer to produce.

"We're talking zero budget here. There was no label, no nothing," McPherson recalls. "I just really wanted to make that record. And so we figured out a way to do it."

You're Dreaming was recorded in the Chicago living room of McPherson's friend, engineer Alex Hall, and it was tracked live — two lead vocals with the band in the same room — which McPherson found a bit terrifying at first. "I couldn't believe how good they were at that," he says. "They actually had to kind of convince me that it was going to be okay."

There are no fiddles on the album, and only sparing use of steel guitar. McPherson wanted to nudge the Cactus Blossoms away from the trap of too much tradition, and the brothers were ready to go past those boundaries. "It was really a big deal for us to have him extend his

offer to help us out," Burkum says of McPherson's producing work. "We needed it. We needed another musician to help take us to where we wanted to go with the new record."

But McPherson emphasizes that he was more of a passenger than a driver. "I was mostly just there as an extra pair of ears and to offer support," he says. "Jack and Page are very, very sure of what they want to do. And if they believe in something, they'll stick to it. I just kind of tried to stay out of the way."

Fast Forward

Before the release of *You're Dreaming*, the Cactus Blossoms played mostly locally, making little tours out of one-off festival dates and the like when they could. But the odometer has been whirling fast in 2016, with dates all around the country, including prime spots opening for Pokey LaFarge and Kacey Musgraves, and a slot at Newport Folk Festival. Despite a few unexpected van repairs and a break-in that was remedied with plywood for a passenger door, Torrey and Burkum were far from road-weary amid their fast-paced schedule last spring.

"We had no idea if our little spaceship would get off the ground," Torrey says. "It's been fun and we've been really busy traveling around and playing shows. ... We're kind of just in a whirlwind of

thinking about if the car's gonna start or not. But it's been really exciting and great. We're really happy that some sad songs can make some other people happy."

On the road, they encounter plenty of questions about what's behind their unique sound, that tinge of timelessness that manages to fit right into the modern world. On the band's website, Torrey explains it as just part of a story that is itself both timeless and modern, the story of a band finding its sound and following where it leads: "That's when the wheel got going and gave the illusion of spinning backwards. We weren't born in the wrong era. We just got into some music from a different era and found a way to make it our own."

Like the stars in the sky, the scent of a rose, or the fit of that favorite pair of jeans, the alchemy of music that reaches across genres, time, and place and into hearts is a mystery — sometimes to artists as much as to their audiences. "We're in the same boat as everybody else," Torrey admits.

"When we hear something back, we're like, 'God, why does that sound kind of old? I was born in 1986, what's going on here?' I think it's just something that comes naturally to us," says Torrey. "We never really thought it was weird until we started to look at it in the context of getting played on the radio ... or getting on some list of new music: we kind of stick out." There's no scheme to it or plan or fetish, it's just fun." ∎

SIBLING
REVELRY

Matthew & Jill Barber join voices to tell the story of a happy family
by Gwendolyn Elliott

IN THE WORLD OF FAMILY BANDS, sibling rivalry is a dynamic that has led to some of the most notorious feuds and public infighting in pop music history (cue the Jacksons, the Gallagher brothers, the Bee Gees). It has its grip in the world of roots music, too, from Carter Family strife to all-out brawls between the Louvin Brothers. And, while always on harmonious terms with his longtime singing partner and sister, Abby, Seattle-based singer-songwriter Noah Gundersen admitted in a recent interview for this journal: "I kind of hate the term 'family band.'"

For Canadian siblings Matthew and Jill Barber — both acclaimed singer-songwriters who have occasionally appeared on each other's records as well as together onstage — singing together is something they've embraced, quite literally, on their first joint project, *The Family Album*.

"For me, it's very personal," Jill says. For 2014's *Fool's Gold*, her most recent solo release and her first after becoming a mom, she says she "didn't want people to feel like I was going soft. I released what I felt was my toughest record yet."

But after making that album, she says, something was missing. "I did have a lot of stuff going on ... that I wanted to put in song, and with a project like this it gave me a platform to write about my family life and to make a record unabashedly about a theme of family. To make this grownup album that wasn't afraid to get a little nostalgic or personal. [With this record, I] wasn't afraid to address the subject of family, which is complex."

"Complex" is an interesting word to use for a brother-sister relationship that from nearly every angle seems as idyllic as could be. With an impeccable reputation in the Canadian music scene, it's perhaps another way of describing, at least for Matthew and Jill, their cozy, familial vibe. "I keep feeling like we need to be giving some dirt," Jill says. "I guess

it would make a better story if there was a lot of rivalry."

But it is true that the subject of family is complicated, and that artistic attempts to celebrate its best qualities often come off sappy. What *The Family Album* provides instead is that rare portrait of two creative souls who not only share the same idea of what it means to be kin, but also have developed a working partnership that actively reveals just what it is: a recognition of a lifelong affection, honored with the skills and abilities they learned, naturally, from one another.

As Jill says, nostalgic and personal are fitting descriptors for *The Family Album*. The inside album image is a photo from a family vacation to Banff, Alberta: Matthew and Jill as two tanned youngsters beside scenic Lake Louise, arms slung around each other, slouched tube socks and all, a picture-perfect portrait of happy childhood.

Good Kids

The Barbers were raised in Port Credit, Ontario, just outside of Toronto. "It was a nice, safe place to grow up, but fairly homogenous and kind of boring," says Matthew, who has since moved to the city with his wife.

"Let me just say I have a new appreciation for it now," says Jill, who resides on the other side of Canada, in Vancouver, with her husband and two kids.

"They were good kids, we never had any problems," recalls their mother, Joyce Barber. "They were very close and they had their alliance against Mom and Dad. I remember when [Matthew] left to go to university, Jill only told me many years later that she was almost bereft for a while because she was 'left alone with Mom and Dad.'"

Joyce adds, "Jillian wanted to do everything that Matthew did."

Matthew, a southpaw, was so much of an influence on young Jill that when she started playing guitar as a teenager, she even adopted his left-handed playing style, which is how she performs on the instrument to this day. "She followed his example on so many things," Joyce says.

"When I was a little kid riding his coattails, he could've easily been like,

'Back off kid, I'm doing my own thing,' but instead he was actually my earliest champion," Jill says. "When I was a 14-year-old girl with lots of feelings, he really encouraged me to put it in song and express myself as a songwriter. I remember it was Matt who gave me Joni Mitchell's *Blue* for Christmas one year, and I have never looked back. Matt's been a big influence on me and we've always been in each other's corner."

"One True Love," the album's rousing third song, was written by Jill and uses this very metaphor.

Tooth and nail I would fight for you
Use my heart like a fist 'till it's black
*   and blue*
When you find your one true love
That is the time, to show what you
*   are made of.*
Get in the ring
Show 'em who you are
Tougher than they think
Each time you raise the bar.

The boxing imagery is ironic, considering Matthew and Jill's closeness, but it echoes some of the challenges that each have faced as solo musicians, and how they've encouraged each other along the way.

"Touring solo can get a little lonely sometimes, and having Jill along is great," Matthew says. "I've had some emotional ups and downs in my career, dealing with my insecurity about my success, about how people see me as an artist. This project is nice in the sense that it feels like a load off having just your name on the marquee or your name on the ticket. Being able to spread out the pressures of putting yourself out there, it just feels like a little weight off the shoulders, because we're sharing it."

"That's what family's for. Sharing the burden," says Jill. "It's hard to make a go of it as a solo artist and be a musician as your career. It takes a lot of individual focus and energy. For the last dozen years or so, Matt and I have each set out with something to prove with each [solo] album, trying to make an impact and to have career momentum. ... I feel a lot less pressure with this record, and I think it made for a better [one]."

The family support doesn't stop there. The singers had just wrapped the first leg of the album's tour when we

> # "I keep feeling like we need to be giving some dirt. I guess it would make a better story if there was a lot of rivalry."
>
> Jill Barber

spoke, and had brought along another family member to help with the logistics of the road: mom (and grandmom) Joyce, acting "tour nanny" for Jill's infant daughter (Jill's husband is on paternity leave at home with their other child).

Joyce isn't a music professional — in fact, she says, her kids always tease her because of how she pronounces Pearl Jam, with something of an upper English accent — but she has been happy to help. "The band is a great group of guys," she says. "They're very accepting of this older lady who's along. Everyone gets along well, so I enjoy it very much. I don't get to see the shows and that's the only thing. There's a TV in the green room, but I'm behind the scenes, looking after the baby.

"Poor Brian," she adds, about her husband, back at home. "He's had to do his own cooking, but he's adapted very well."

A Lifetime in the Making

Jill sings in a smoky alto that recalls Norah Jones, though when it soars, it takes on the shape of Alison Krauss' fluttering twang. It's a tone well-adapted to the various expressions of jazz, rock, pop, and country she explores in her many solo releases. But her particular fondness for torch songs (2008's Juno-nominated *Chances*, co-written with Canadian songwriter Ron Sexsmith), classic French standards (2013's *Chansons*), and large-living originals with cues from the great songbook of '60s pop appears to be tracing an arc similar to that of fellow Canadian chanteuse Diana Krall.

Matthew's style is more loose, rollicking, and rootsy. He's cut records with

Gary Louris of the Jayhawks (2014's tender, measured *Big Romance*), scored the songs for a slightly raunchy musical, *Haunted Hillbilly*, and produced arrangements that recall new and old classic acts, from Wilco to Tom Petty. Early on, his voice had an easy, breezy quality not unlike Jack Johnson, though his pipes in later albums take on a pure and mellow tone that conjure visions of Jackson Browne.

The Family Album was recorded at Union Sound Studios in Toronto by noted engineer Chris Stringer (The Wooden Sky, Elliott Brood, Timber Timbre, Holly McNarland) and mixed by Michael Piersante, whose work on Robert Plant and Alison Krauss' *Raising Sand* won him a Grammy. In fact, *The Family Album* is styled in a similar way to *Raising Sand*, a collection of beloved folk covers. And like that recording, it even includes an adaptation of Townes Van Zandt, in this case the aching classic, "If I Needed You." In addition to its six cover songs, they contributed five originals, two written by Matthew and three by Jill.

The album was a lifetime in the making, the duo says, though perhaps the most unique thing about Matthew and Jill's musical path is that, unlike so many family bands, they weren't raised by musical parents.

"It was important for both Joyce and I that they had musical opportunity, a foundation that neither of us had," says Brian. "We never had music lessons when we were growing up. We were just certain that it would be more enriching for them if they had an opportunity for formal instruction of a certain sort." Thus, both received piano lessons, but "we both quit," Jill says.

Mom and Dad Barber remember a slightly different version of the story. Matthew, Brian says, who was far more into hockey at the time, "was kind of fired by his piano teacher." As any sibling would, Matthew lumps little sis into the situation. "I don't think the piano lessons, the practicing and learning scales, really stuck with either Jill or I."

He says their true talents emerged instead by feeling and learning by ear. "That's kind of the way we operate. I don't think we're embarrassed of that, in fact it could be one of those things that sustains you through a career in music. Sometimes people can feel suffocated with the theory side of it at a young age and never go back to music."

Even though Joyce and Brian Barber aren't musicians themselves, their influence looms large on *The Family Album*. Back when both Barber siblings were Pearl Jam fans, Neil Young was one of the only artists the whole family could agree on. "We're both from Winnipeg, both Brian and I," says Joyce. "We always had an affinity for [Neil Young], and so did the kids." In fact, Young's song, "Comes a Time," closes the record.

"It's completely unexpected how this has all turned out," Brian says. "I was mentioning to them yesterday, in an email, another one of the songs on *The Family Album* is 'Summer Wages' by Ian & Sylvia, who were a folk duo back in the day, in the '60s and '70s. Joyce and I went out to see them during our university years at the University of Manitoba student union building. And to think that it's now 50 years later that my kids are singing the same songs that we heard back then … is quite surprising to me, and amazing. It also has a feeling of continuity about it all." ∎

Sean Ardoin.

PARDON MY FRENCH

Creole sounds find new life in Louisiana's Ardoin family

by Megan Romer

Bois Sec Ardoin on his farm in Eunice, Louisiana.

"I DON'T EVEN SAY I PLAY ZYDECO anymore," says Sean Ardoin, a scion of one of the first families of zydeco. Considering his family line and his predilection for the accordion, it's a surprising statement. But then he goes on: "People think they know what zydeco is. They think it's whatever it was they first heard, but really, it's like they drank strawberry Kool-Aid. You drink strawberry Kool-Aid and then taste a real strawberry for the first time, you're going to think, 'What is this?' It's totally unfamiliar and they can't make sense of it."

Of course, the music of the francophone black Creoles in South Louisiana is not and never has been a static genre. Like the wheezing bellows of the accordion — which has anchored its sound for over a century — the music pushes and pulls, inhaling influences out of everything from old field hollers to Baton Rouge rapper Lil Boosie, breathing its own life into sounds as different as trad Cajun music and Paul Simon's *Graceland*. The Ardoin family story is as inextricable from this music as Creole identity is inextricable from the Ardoin family.

Frequently, label heads and music promoters — and even academics who should know better — have described zydeco as being Cajun music with an African influence. They tend to explain that it is rooted in European folk tradition, which emphasizes story-telling over form, with added elements of African tradition, which they characterize as

being focused on rhythm and dance. This explanation diminishes the fact that traditional Cajun music — which came from the descendants of white Acadians who settled in South Louisiana after expulsion from Canada in 1755 — is largely a string-driven dance-based music, and African music is as broad and diverse as the continent itself. But in a place where "Cajun" has become as much a catch-phrase for Baton Rouge bureaucrats and New Orleans tourism officials as it is a 400-year-old cultural identity, Creole culture has, in the narrative sold to outsiders, become subsumed and overwhelmed by the Cajun culture.

Nonetheless, you'd be hard-pressed to find a Cajun or Creole who couldn't explain the difference to you. "It's black and white," exclaims Lawrence "Black" Ardoin, Sean's father. "That's the easiest way I can explain it."

Distant Roots

Cajun and Creole cultures arose in the same place: the bayou-laced prairies and swamps of South Louisiana, outside the urban centers of New Orleans and Baton Rouge. Each culture borrowed from the other, while also maintaining its own distinct identity. Black Creoles were part of a greater Franco-American network of Creoles that lived in the area stretching from Mobile through New Orleans, as far north as Natchez and Natchitoches. They were, in the antebellum period, known as gens de couleur libres (free people of color). They were the country cousins — and business associates and marriage prospects — of the Creoles in the bigger cities and settlements. They were planters who owned sometimes significant property, both real and chattel, including human property. They were, of course, almost entirely descended from enslaved people themselves, mostly via concubinages between French or Spanish men and enslaved women of color.

The majority of Louisiana's enslaved population during the colonial period was brought from Senegambia (now Senegal and The Gambia), and they were largely Bambara, a Mandé people who still thrive in Mali and neighboring countries.

Bambara people are known for their jeli — a caste of griots who play stringed

instruments and maintain historical records of their villages and people via epic poem-songs, some of which are hundreds of verses long. Their American-born (i.e., the very definition of "Creole") offspring would, and still do, carry on this tradition through their powerful story-songs. Heavier African polyrhythms — mostly derived from smaller-but-still-influential numbers of Yoruba and Kongo people, as well as Haitian music traditions from the post-rebellion exodus of both black and white people to Louisiana — contributed to this mix.

Meanwhile, French-derived string-band traditions — and circle, square, and couple dancing — were also unquestionably a key element of Creole music and culture. Some of these traditions descended directly from France and other European countries through direct settlers, and others came through the Acadian-descended small farmers and fishermen who neighbored black Creole planters before the Civil War. Still more crossed color lines during the antebellum period of sharecropping. At that time, the white Cajuns — as well as economically devastated Creoles of color — worked alongside liberated black folks in a sharecropper system that took over the region at the expense of just about everyone who wasn't white and already wealthy. Incidentally, this era also saw a fair amount of crossover between family bloodlines, in one way or another, which explains the Ardoin family's Acadian surname.

The shared language, as well as shared Catholic faith — otherwise rare in the rural South — were keystones. By the time the Great Depression and the Second World War rolled around, race relations were less than ideal, but still kinder than those between "les français" (francophones) and "les américains" (anglophones), and certainly better than elsewhere in the Deep South. The differences between "black Creoles" (francophone descendants of enslaved people) and "Creoles of color" (francophone descendants of free people of color) faded slowly via intermarriages and the simple passage of time. The Civil Rights Movement of the 1950s and '60s did away with it entirely, ushering in pride in shared African heritage to all but a few holdouts.

L to R: Bois Sec Ardoin and Canray Fontenot
playing on the National Mall, Washington, DC.

Despite concurrent-but-separate cultural histories being easily traced via historical record, the popular record tends to ascribe any cultural innovations to the Cajun people, often with subtle insinuations that all people of African descent ever did was beat some drums. Sure, the complexities are hard to describe succinctly, but they're often explained just plain inaccurately. Even the state's own "Louisiana Soundtrack" music website, designed to promote musical tourism to the state, states that "Early zydeco was a blend of Louisiana French accordion music and Afro-Caribbean beats."

Adding the Accordion

"The black people, the Creoles, they got the accordion first," Sean Ardoin explains. "They had it for a good 20 years, maybe longer, before Cajun people even started playing it. The Cajuns were all playing stringband music at that point. Cajuns playing accordion — that all came later. It all came from Amédé Ardoin. [In fact,] the whole traditional Cajun repertoire comes from Amédé. It's not the other way around. What they call 'Cajun music' — that all comes from us."

Amédé Ardoin, a distant cousin of today's Ardoin family, simply referred to the music he made as "French music" or "la musique Français." Ardoin was not the first black Creole musician recorded, but he was by far the most influential, both in his time — the 1920s and '30s — and throughout the ensuing decades. A tiny man, standing around five feet tall, he was a notorious rambler, flirt, and bon vivant.

"They didn't like him, his family. He never worked," explains Lawrence Ardoin, Sean's father. "He just rode around in his horse and buggy with the reins wrapped around his legs, steering, and playing his accordion the whole time." But he played beautifully and sang even better — a plaintive, bluesy voice that notoriously brought women to tears as he moaned out the sad laments of unrequited and lost love that became his trademark.

Amédé recorded 34 tracks from 1929 to 1934, but he was best known in the communities in and around Eunice, Louisiana, for playing house parties, often alongside white fiddler Dennis McGee. "The black people in those days didn't have any money," Lawrence says, "so they mostly only got paid for playing for white people. And they'd play for the white people until midnight, or whenever

the white people were ready to let them go. Then they'd want to keep playing, so they'd go on over and play for the black people until everyone was too tired."

Young Bois Sec Ardoin, Lawrence's father and a distant relative of Amédé ("Daddy always said 'cousin,' but it wasn't really close," explains Lawrence), would slip out to some of these later dances and watch Amédé play, learning everything he could.

Like so many genre pioneers, Amédé met a tragic ending. The family story is that one hot, late night while playing a barn dance, Amédé called for a handkerchief or a towel. One of the young daughters of the white man who owned the farm handed him her hankie. In some versions of the tale, she even wiped his face herself. Regardless, the good ol' boys watching the scene didn't take kindly to the interaction, and when the dance was done, they beat Amédé severely, leaving him with brain injuries and internal bleeding. For all that race relations were moderately better in French Louisiana than in neighboring Mississippi or Texas, there were still social rules, and Amédé had broken a big one.

His brain injuries led to a severe mental deterioration — Amédé, who was probably in his late 30s at the time of the beating, was said to have lost the ability

L to R: Clarence Leday, Ed Poullard, Donald Caesar, Lawrence Ardoin, Paul Thomas, Dallas Deville, Russell Ardoin.

to play music and even to care for himself. "But his family, remember, they didn't like him because he was kind of a drifter the whole time," Lawrence says, "and he didn't have a wife or kids, so it was off to Pineville."

"Pineville" was the state insane asylum, and Amédé lived out his final two months of life there in 1942. He was buried in the hospital cemetery.

"I went to look for his grave," Lawrence continues. "I went three different times to try to find the records. They took me out there and showed me the field where they buried them. They said, 'Everything on this side, that's the Caucasians. Everything on this side, that's the African-Americans.' In those days, they just marked the grave with a wooden cross that had a number, no gravestone. They tried to find the records for me to find where he was, but they were all gone. I went three times, but couldn't find it." He shakes his head.

"Not even a name," Sean adds. "Just a number. They kept [black folks and white folks] apart, even in death."

Ironic then, that Amédé's legacy has largely been kept alive by traditional Cajun musicians. His songs entered the repertoire via Iry LeJeune, a visually impaired Cajun accordion player who, unable to farm because of his eyesight,

learned all of Amédé's songs from records. LeJeune re-recorded them — re-titled, re-arranged, and occasionally with new sets of lyrics — in the late 1940s and early '50s.

These punchy, powerful recordings, peppered heavily with the spirited "Aieeeee!" that is so readily associated with Cajun music, went on to become canonical for Cajun musicians to this day. Then, in yet another of the tragic tales that saturate the story of Louisiana music, LeJeune was killed in a car accident at age 26, struck while helping a friend change a tire on the side of the road.

That Griot Gene

Bois Sec Ardoin, the aforementioned father of Lawrence and distant cousin and musical protégé of Amédé, was a contemporary of LeJeune's. He earned his unusual nickname (it means "dry wood") from his childhood talent for getting to the barn quickly when rainstorms rolled across the fields. It was around age 12 that Bois Sec got hold of his brother's accordion, which he'd sneak into the hayloft to practice.

"Well, you know, that didn't work so good with an accordion — they're loud," laughs Lawrence. Lawrence learned

much later, after Bois Sec had died, that the instrument had originally belonged to Bois Sec's father, who died during the Spanish flu epidemic in 1919, when Bois Sec was a toddler. He had never played it out in public, but had, apparently, played it well.

Bois Sec's musical partner of nearly 50 years was fiddler Canray Fontenot, who was also the son of an accordion player. But his father, "Nonc" Adam Fontenot, played far and wide. Canray was a wildly dynamic, bluesy fiddler who drank heavily but who had, as Lawrence puts it, "a mind like a trap. He could tell you the same story one day, and turn around and tell it to you 50 years later and not a thing would change."

Sean interrupts: "He had that griot gene." Indeed, listening to early Bois Sec and Canray recordings and comparing the ones from many decades later, it's easy to hear the songs change musically over time, shifting slightly in form, length, and speed. Canray's lyrics, though, never waver.

A decade after Clifton Chenier burst onto the national folk music scene playing a new genre called "zydeco" — that urbane blend of traditional French music and electrified rhythm and blues — Ralph Rinzler and some other scouts from the Newport Folk Festival came looking for more traditional Louisiana French musicians. They found Bois Sec and Canray, who agreed to come play their "la-la music," but who refused to fly. So in 1966, the year after Bob Dylan took to the same stage with an electric band, Ardoin and Fontenot made the trip from Duralde, Louisiana, to Newport, Rhode Island, by car. They played unaccompanied, a slate of traditional waltzes, two-steps, blues, and laments. It's hard to say exactly how the crowd reacted, but video shows the two looking comfortable, smiling and foot-tapping their way through their sets.

Rinzler was one of the first national folklorists to come digging through the treasure trove of Creole musicians, but he was far from the last. "Oh yeah, that guy Alan Lomax? Yeah, my mama slapped him," laughs Lawrence, recalling an incident in the church hall in Duralde. "He was down visiting for a few months, doing some filming, and they was all at the church hall. I don't know what he said to her, but — pow!"

Of Bois Sec's 14 children, several played music, first behind their father, and then in the Ardoin Brothers band. During the 1970s, there was a bit of a lull in the scene. It's hard to say exactly why, but it coincided with a lot of modernization in Louisiana: an oil boom, for one, and the completion of Interstate 10, which finally made a quick and easy connection from Houston through Lake Charles, Lafayette, and Baton Rouge to New Orleans. The music wasn't dead, but it was a down time for sure, and another boom wouldn't come until the early '80s.

Even with the changes during that time period, there were still people who wanted to dance, and there was music that needed to be kept breathing. The Ardoin Brothers were perhaps the most dedicated musical journeymen of this era. They played dances weekly, spreading the music across a broader area than most bands before them had done. Brother Morris Ardoin started his own small dancehall near their father's place in Duralde. Lawrence, who had moved to Lake Charles to work as a mechanic, held dances and revived a "chicken run" Mardi Gras tradition that is credited as the precursor to the now-massive Creole trail ride scene. Trail rides take place every weekend, except for the hottest few weeks of the year, and consist of hundreds of people on

horseback riding a pre-planned trail, later meeting up for a large dance and cookout. Trail rides have, according to Sean, largely replaced the club scene as the place to go for zydeco music.

By the late '80s, Lawrence was leading his own band, which featured rhythm powerhouse son Sean on drums and occasionally a song or two by Sean's 11-years-younger brother, Chris, on accordion. As the next decade rolled in, Lawrence was noticing he more frequently hung up his accordion. "They wanted to hear zydeco — Keith Frank and Andrus [Esprit, better known as Beau Jocque]. The la-la just wasn't getting 'em out anymore," he recalls. Nonetheless, his sons were ready to step into the spotlight and take on the family business. Lawrence moved into a managerial role and Sean stepped up, taking on the lion's share of songwriting and vocal duties from his seat at the drum kit. Chris handled accordion duties in their new band, called Double Clutchin' after the style of kick-drumming that is the hallmark of modern zydeco. With this configuration, the brothers' careers careened into something that is as close to superstardom as zydeco musicians are likely to get.

Always Been Modern

Chris Ardoin is a quiet, shy man, but he is unashamed about his use of contemporary African-American sounds in his music. A powerful singer, he's still happy to occasionally use Auto-Tune or other voice modifiers for effect. He duets with rappers and Louisiana R&B stars like Cupid. His songs bear as much of the imprint of urban radio as they do that of his distant cousin Amédé, and his Creole crowds love him for it. They pack the tents at weekly trail rides and fill clubs to capacity every time he plays.

Or, at least, the locals love it. Out-of-state crowds? Not so much. "When Chris and these other guys play those sets outside the state, at the folk festivals, they play a more traditional set," explains Sean. The largely white audiences at these events are turned off by the effects Chris brings to the music — the hip-hop, the modernism. Sean laughs about it. "There's no explaining to them that it's a genre that has always been modern."

Sean Ardoin took an extended break from music in the early 2000s but has come back to it in the past few years. "I don't want to mess around," he says. "I'm here to work smarter, not harder." He sees a niche in the club scene, which has been largely abandoned in favor of the insular community trail rides, and he sees it being filled by white pseudo-zydeco bands. "People will say 'Oh, these new bands, they're so cool, they play zydeco, but they also incorporate rock and funk and reggae.' Please. We've been doing that since before these kids were out of high school. They just weren't paying attention.

"That's why I don't say that I play zydeco anymore," he adds. "I say 'zydeco,' and they have a preconceived notion. It's that strawberry Kool-Aid. I call it 'Alternative Creole' now, which lets me have my space to do what I want to."

Part of what he wants to do is — as always — to modernize the music, to update the tradition. As well as being a strong songwriter, Sean has a gift for unexpected covers. A YouTube search reveals clever zydeco covers of Adele's "Hello" and Drake's "Hotline Bling." but it was his zydeco cover of Pharrell's "Happy" that caught the ear of the Lake Charles tourism board, which has used the song in promotions.

That's a bit ironic, given that, in Lawrence's words, "They shut down our Creole Mardi Gras. It's so expensive to have dances now at the Lake Charles Civic Center, because they make us hire cops — six or eight of them at $35 an hour. And they make it a hassle with permits. It's not worth it! You can't make any money with that."

When asked why they have to hire so much security, he simply gestures to his skin. The commodification of Creole cultural output at the expense of actual support of Creole communities is, it seems, alive and well. And the racism that got Amédé beaten senseless so long ago has, as in so many places, shifted from the interpersonal to something more systemic. When asked if this particular update on another old tradition is discouraging, Sean guffaws.

"Nah!" he says. "None of this has stopped us yet. We're always going to keep making music, and doing it the way we want." ∎

Lawrence Ardoin (on accordion) performing with members of the Ardoin Brothers Band.

"People will say 'Oh, these new bands, they're so cool, they play zydeco, but they also incorporate rock and funk and reggae.' Please. We've been doing that since before these kids were out of high school. They just weren't paying attention." —Sean Ardoin

Ani DiFranco, who moved to New Orleans from Buffalo, New York, a little over a decade ago, with the Preservation Hall Jazz Band.

STEINWAY & SONS

DINO PERRUCCI

**Modern roots
artists stoke
the spirit of
New Orleans**
by Allison Moorer

NATIVES AND NEWCOMERS

MUSIC IS A WAY OF LIFE IN New Orleans. It's everywhere — on the streets where you might happen upon a second line, a jazz funeral, or a busker; in the bars where you might hear young, unparalleled talent just nearing full bloom or a legend holding an audience rapt. It's in the gardens, trees, and flowers. It's in the shotgun houses, Creole cottages, and stately, double gallery homes. It even lives in the graveyards, which rise in every ward like melancholy cities of the dead. It doesn't matter where you go — Jackson Square, Frenchmen Street, Gentilly, the Ninth Ward, Marigny, Bywater, Tremé, the French Quarter, or on to the Garden District and Uptown — you can feel it in the damp air that settles around your shoulders and in the soggy ground beneath your feet.

When you consider America's myriad music scenes, there isn't another one as distinctive. Of course, it's a singular city to start with. There, French, Spanish, African, and Deep South cultures collide to create a lusty, lively, sybaritic environment that most people find hard not to love. Or maybe it's the music that makes the city so special — it is, after all, the Crescent City's saving grace.

Music in New Orleans is alive; it feels like freedom. Where there is freedom, there is imagination. Where there is imagination, there is possibility and promise. Naturally, musicians the world over are drawn to the city's unique energy, undeniable beauty, hint of danger, and insouciance. Luke Winslow-King certainly was, though he was raised in Michigan.

A singer, songwriter, and guitarist who deftly mixes tradition and modernity, Winslow-King found himself stranded in New Orleans at 19 years old after his touring vehicle was stolen.

"We left our car parked in front of this pink hotel, and I've been here since," he says. "Before I came to New Orleans,

I had been studying jazz and classical music in school. So for me, there were two different kinds of music: the kind you learned in school and the people's music — Woody Guthrie and stuff like that. When I came to New Orleans, I discovered traditional jazz, and there was a kind of improvisational [approach to] people's music here. You could sing and dance to it. There was collective improvisation, where everyone is playing all at once. I saw my two worlds collide.

"I also liked the tropical nature of the city," he adds. "There's music everywhere and people have that Southern charm and hospitality that I hadn't really experienced before in the North."

That hospitality is another key to the city's powerful pull.

"I had a really warm welcome to the city by legendary jazz singer John Boutte," Winslow-King remembers. "He introduced me to a lot of great musicians during my first few weeks here. I was really lucky to have a great introduction."

It's true that many music scenes can be quite protective of their inner circles, and there's always been a lean toward exclusivity in New Orleans, when it comes to supposed carpetbaggers hawking the locals' tones and tunes. But if you have something real to put forth, the city's doors are wide open.

"After Hurricane Katrina," Winslow-King says, "the city flooded with new talent, and a lot of people [were] interested in being part of the music scene here, which kind of changed the city. I think overall it's a pretty inclusive place. If you come here with an open mind and you have something to offer, I think you'll definitely be embraced."

Soak Up the Joy

New Orleans has always had its own identity and agenda — musically and otherwise. Maybe because it's such a hybrid in the first place, its music has never required much outside influence, but outsiders have always added to it anyway. There's never a shortage of musicians who take up residence there in hopes of absorbing the magic, at least some of the mayhem, and ultimately try to contribute in some way. Most of all it seems they want to soak up the joy —

to pass a good time while experiencing the satisfaction of playing music for music's sake, in a place where it's a life force, a nonsalable accompaniment to birth, death, and everything in between.

Music in general is non-negotiable to the spirit, and no city's people know that better than New Orleanians.

Ben Jaffe certainly knows it. His parents, Allan and Sandra Jaffe, founded Preservation Hall in 1961 to help keep traditional New Orleans jazz thriving. They raised their son in the French Quarter, at the feet of countless legends. The younger Jaffe is now creative director of his parents' esteemed venue.

"New Orleans is my home," he says. "I was born and raised here. It's in my DNA. New Orleans is like no other place I've been. There's a reason why so much incredible music originated there. The unique blending of cultures and traditions led to the advent of jazz. Every artist must make their pilgrimage to New Orleans and walk the streets of Jelly Roll Morton and King Oliver and Louis Armstrong and Fats Domino and Dave Bartholomew and Allen Toussaint.

"Music is a reflection of our community and our community is a reflection of our music," he adds. "The two are inseparable. The music I grew up with served a function; it serves a purpose. The purpose is to bring joy and uplift the city's spirit. That ingredient is ever-present. Food feeds our body, but music fuels our soul. We wouldn't be New Orleans without our musical traditions."

Jaffe welcomes those who come to the city to immerse themselves in its character and essence, as well as make it their home. "Newcomers bring a fresh perspective that can be inspiring," he says. "Outsiders often see things that are lost when you see the world from the inside-out as opposed to the outside-in. Outsiders bring their own traditions and identity."

Nonetheless, not everyone who tries to assimilate thrives in New Orleans. These are the streets where Buddy Bolden, who some say invented jazz but was inarguably its first bona fide star, supposedly lost his mind during a parade in 1906. The history of New Orleans is full of such stories. It can be a hard, haunted place. For every pleasantry and lagniappe, New Orleans has its antithesis.

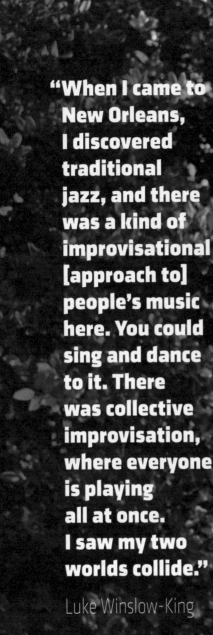

"When I came to New Orleans, I discovered traditional jazz, and there was a kind of improvisational [approach to] people's music here. You could sing and dance to it. There was collective improvisation, where everyone is playing all at once. I saw my two worlds collide."

Luke Winslow-King

"A lot of people love New Orleans, but New Orleans doesn't always love you back," Jaffe says. "New Orleans can be beautiful, but it can also chew you up and spit you out. If you submit yourself to the city and come with an open heart and humility, New Orleans will embrace you as one of its own. But you cannot be at odds with it. You will lose that battle every time. You must accept her with all her beauty and pitfalls and shortcomings. There's also a dark side to this city. We are a port town with 24-hour bars. If you are predisposed, New Orleans can be a cruel, cruel place."

Weathering the Storm

Perhaps one of the cruelest times the Crescent City has seen — and one of the most important displays of its strength and character — was the aftermath of Hurricane Katrina in 2005. Musicians were displaced from their homes — some permanently. Prized instruments that had been in families for generations were lost. Countless, priceless recordings and archives drowned in the dirty, brackish water that flooded the homes, clubs, and studios that held so much of the city's culture and history. All those who remained could do was pull the parts back together into a somehow strengthened sum.

"We collectively experienced something profound," Jaffe offers. "And that very rarely happens. Katrina brought us closer together. There is a survivor's pride

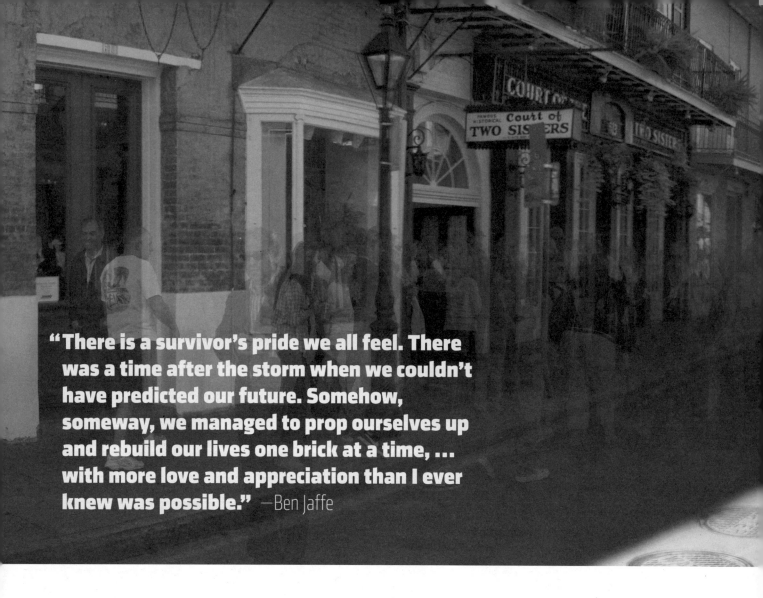

"There is a survivor's pride we all feel. There was a time after the storm when we couldn't have predicted our future. Somehow, someway, we managed to prop ourselves up and rebuild our lives one brick at a time, … with more love and appreciation than I ever knew was possible." —Ben Jaffe

we all feel. There was a time after the storm when we couldn't have predicted our future. Somehow, someway, we managed to prop ourselves up and rebuild our lives one brick at a time, stronger than we were before, with more love and appreciation than I ever knew was possible."

Music held New Orleans together and it rebounded, but as it continues to heal it can't help but be changed. The disaster opened New Orleans' doors wider, sparking a renewal of traditions as well as an even deeper appreciation and embrace of the city's backbone. But gentrification always alters not only the physical landscape but the emotional and artistic ones as well.

Artists of all disciplines have traditionally been able to keep afloat without too much struggle due to the low cost of living, easygoing attitude, and no lack of inspiring fodder all around the city.

Earning a living as a professional musician has always been something to be respected, even revered. But, Winslow-King admits, "It's getting harder as more and more musicians come. I've been really blessed. I worked my way up from the bottom and I'm really lucky to have great gigs and great support here in the city now. You can make a living here, but you can do that anywhere. It's just like Austin or Nashville or New York. Nothing's free."

What those other music towns lack, however, is the level of collaboration and cross-pollination that's become more likely — and more necessary — since Katrina. Where musicians once found it easy to stay inside their own categories, there's now more reaching and an ever-expanding melting pot of styles. Everyone is more open to playing with everyone now, and there's a heartier welcome from the Yats (locals) to the inconnus (outsiders), or those who might have once been considered interlopers.

Jaffe considers this essential to keeping the music alive and progressing at Preservation Hall. "We're going to continue to seek out collaborators," he says. "It's become part of who we are and what we do. I love introducing new artists to Preservation Hall and New Orleans. I love the moment an artist visits the Hall for the first time. You can see their brain try to process the whole experience. It's amazing to be part of that process."

Winslow-King is also encouraged to mix it up. "People stick to their genre, but there is crossover in the hip-hop and brass band scenes for sure," he says. "There's crossover in the traditional jazz and country scenes. There's definitely crossover where it makes sense."

Groundbreaking musician, singer-songwriter, poet, and activist Ani

DiFranco was born and raised in Buffalo, New York, but settled in New Orleans in 2003. She, too, says the opportunities for collaboration are "endless."

Asked what drew her to the Crescent City, DiFranco doesn't hesitate: "You mean besides it being a musical mecca? New Orleans is where people of all stripes come to set themselves free and musicians and freaks can make a living. Alcohol and debauchery fuel the game but also there are powerful ghosts on hand to shake you to your core."

Indeed, what is music without at least a little mysticism? New Orleans' music and mystique can't always be understood; you have to be inside it to feel it, and give yourself over to it to get it. The amaranthine mystery of the city is akin to the best of songs: charming, beguiling, beautiful, stirring, sometimes a little unhinged, and utterly romantic.

You want to play it over and over — it never gets old. You want to stay inside the perfectly imperfect, glorious, sexy place that only it can take you to.

In a world that's becoming more for sale every day, at lower and lower prices, it's no wonder that those who want to root themselves in something that resists the faux and embraces the fais do-do would head south. There's no such thing as flawless or faultless, and New Orleans certainly isn't either, but it does have soul and inspiration in spades.

What inspires DiFranco about New Orleans, she says, is "the architecture and the physical spaces. The live oak trees. The realness of the people and the slowness of their walk." Winslow-King adds that no other locale could provide for him what his adopted hometown does.

"For me, I think the music business is definitely thriving a lot more in Nashville,

New York, and L.A., and that's appealing," he says. "But the reason that I'll stay in New Orleans is because there's camaraderie. The support I get from the community and the soul in the music, I don't think you can find anywhere else.

"I feel like Nashville music is a commodity. In New York, music is a business. ... In New Orleans, music is part of life," he adds. "You may get paid for a gig, but the music's not for sale. It's something that people keep in their hearts and keep as a part of their identity and as a passion in their life. For me, that's what keeps me here. It keeps me grounded in the soul of the music. That's the root of why I create music and why I became an artist, and what I believe at a spiritual level. The way people revere music and treat it as part of the culture [in New Orleans] is really special. It keeps my music genuine and authentic." ■

INHERITED FROM THE LAND

Music pours out of Mississippi

by Lee Zimmerman

Luther Dickinson.

"THE MISSISSIPPI SOUND IS ALL about soul," says Luther Dickinson, and he should know. As a co-founder, with his brother Cody, of the North Mississippi Allstars, Dickinson can claim those muddy roots as part of his DNA. And as the son of Jim Dickinson, one of the most influential producers in the annals of roots music, Luther is well aware of the heritage that accompanies the state he calls home.

"It's about the roots of American music," he continues. "It's about gospel music, about people in the fields, people singing to themselves and sharing it with others. It's about community. ... It's all about the American dream and about the different cultures. Even though they were separated by segregation, the music brought people together and it became a beautiful thing. It created rock and roll and R&B and soul music, and it turned gospel music into a sexy, secular phenomenon."

Indeed, Mississippi's musical legacy is among the richest and most resilient in the nation, one that rivals Texas, Tennessee, California, and New York. It's a history that goes back to the early 18th century, borne of brutal racism and deep hardship as it offered hope and opportunity for those who figured out that music can be a path toward liberation and, eventually, opportunity.

The music that evolved into the blues was birthed in the farm fields of the Mississippi Delta, where slaves chanted in rhythm and shared their sorrows, expressing misery and finding strength for their toil. After the Civil War, as slavery gave way to Reconstruction, Mississippi's music culture developed form and structure, eventually coalescing into songs. Traces of African music, brought to America through the slave trade, remained a prominent part of the mix. And Southern Mississippi became the breeding ground for the blues, well before the form moved north to Memphis and Chicago, or west to New Orleans.

"It's all a part of our history," says Garrad Lee, one of the owners of Mississippi-based music label Homework Town Records. Lee is also a principal in the Jackson, Mississippi, production company Elegant Trainwreck and a local DJ. "All American music can be traced back to the plantations. Work songs, spirituals, chants, and the rest gave birth to the blues, and everything branches off that. What makes Mississippi so fertile is the history behind the music and the broad tastes of the people in the state who consume the music."

"Mississippi is midway between Memphis and New Orleans — two cities that are rich in Southern culture," notes Dickinson, whose new solo album, *Blues and Ballads*, celebrates that sharing of traditional tunes from one generation to another. "The connection between [those two cities] is Mississippi. I always maintain that it's the people that make a place great, and it's the people that have passed the tradition down, person to person, hand to hand."

Indeed, those who championed the music early on — Charlie Patton, Son House, and Robert Johnson among them — became key proponents of this evolving musical form, laying the foundation that fellow Mississippians such as Willie Dixon, B.B. King, Howlin' Wolf, Muddy Waters, Mississippi John Hurt, Sonny Boy Williamson, Fred McDowell, Elmore James, Bukka White, John Lee Hooker, Albert King, Junior Kimbrough, Big Joe Williams, Otis Clay, Big Bill Broonzy, Otis Spann, Hubert Sumlin, Furry Lewis, and James Cotton would build on decades later. Immortalized in song, the towns of Clarksdale, Rosedale, Vicksburg, and Biloxi became familiar signposts for musical pilgrims.

The blues has always thrived in Mississippi, from its formal beginnings in the 1890s to its prime in the 1920s and '30s. Roadhouses — or, as they were known locally, "juke joints" — began to spring up along the state's highways and in countless small towns, providing gathering spots for itinerant musicians to share their songs and learn technique from others. Although the lure of the big city would eventually claim King, Dixon, Wolf, Lewis, James, and others, many of whom would later be signed by Chicago's iconic Chess Records, the influence of these Mississippi masters left an indelible imprint on the state as well as the entire trajectory of American music.

Singer Johnny Rawls can attest to that. Born and raised in Mississippi, he recalls what it was like growing up in its vibrant musical scene. "I could walk down the street and hear people singing their hearts out," he remembers. "There were blues bands and soul bands everywhere. I never realized what a blessing it was. It was so natural, like putting your shoes on. It was nothing special to me then, but now I look back and realize how blessed I was to be able to witness some of the greatest singers who ever walked the earth. I look back and think, 'Wow. Who would ever get an opportunity like that?'"

It *was* an opportunity, but Rawls also knows it was something more. "It's spiritual," he suggests. "It was nothing that was planned. It came out of hardship and oppression. There were people there that you may never have heard of, but they had the real deal when it came to their sound. You can't really explain it. They just have it. You can't find it anywhere else but there. They inherited it from the land, from the earth, from their struggles."

The Mississippi Sound

"What they call Mississippi sound migrated to Chicago, and the people got more slick and educated on what to play and how to play, and then learned to play better," reflects bluesman Bobby Rush. "Now they talk about Chicago blues ... but that's only a guy from Mississippi that learned to play better.

"Making love, being in love, being up, being down, being broke, having heartaches and pain — they all relate the same way," Rush continues. "All blues is pretty much the same. ... That's why Mississippi is so strong. It all started here. This was the root of it all. You have Blind Lemon, Muddy Waters, B.B. King, Fats Domino, Robert Johnson, and all the guys I can think of in my time, before my time, and even before my daddy's time. They were speaking and singing the blues."

Still, Mississippi can claim credit for more than just the birth of the blues. In many ways the music that the state fostered led to a sound that would

"It all started here. This was the root of it all. You have Blind Lemon, Muddy Waters, B.B. King, Fats Domino, Robert Johnson, and all the guys I can think of in my time, before my time, and even before my daddy's time. They were speaking and singing the blues."

Bobby Rush

proliferate far beyond its borders: a phenomenon that became known as rock and roll.

"Mississippi is a conundrum wrapped in an enigma," explains singer-songwriter Jimbo Mathus, whose latest album *Band of Storms* (released last spring) reflects his home state's multi-hued tradition. "It's this very mystery — always held close to the vest by its initiates — that has created the legacy born of the suffering known as the blues.

"The blues had a baby and they named it rock and roll," he adds. "Visionaries such as Sam Phillips had the wisdom and fearlessness to behold the vision, use the white man bwana bwana to make recordings translatable to the masses, and — voila — Elvis."

Ah, Elvis. Born in tiny Tupelo, Mississippi, Presley remains the state's most famous son — the man who brought rock and roll to the masses and forever changed the course of modern music. But he's hardly the only Mississippian that's cast an eternal influence. Artists as diverse as jazzman Mose Allison, composer John Luther Adams, producer/songwriter Glen Ballard, gospel singers the Blackwood Brothers, rock and soul fusionists the Chambers Brothers, rocker Delaney Bramlett, tropical troubadour Jimmy Buffett, rock and roll pioneer Bo Diddley, country stars Bobbie Gentry, Charlie Pride, Conway Twitty, Marty Stuart, Jimmie Rodgers, LeAnn Rimes, Faith Hill, and Mickey Gilley, soul singers Jimmy Ruffin and Thelma Houston, studio stalwart Lloyd Green, Burrito Brother Chris Ethridge, gospel great

Mylon LeFevre, and former Supreme Mary Wilson are just a few who can claim a Mississippi birthright. And happily, many of those native sons and daughters remain an integral part of the state's musical legacy.

"The hill country blues changed my life," Dickinson says. "It's primitive modernism and that's why I love it. That's what rock and roll is all about. It's young white dudes playing the blues. ... It's American poetry that goes back from generation to generation, all open to interpretation. You keep it permanent, but you do your thing and hopefully that will allow Mississippi music to live on."

Adding to the Mix

In the '70s and '80s, the Mississippi music scene reinvented itself, and while blues still remained as vital as ever, the infusion of pop, roots-rock, and other more contemporary sounds began to take hold in the musical firmament. Bands like the Hilltops, Blue Mountain, and the Windbreakers hinted at a greater sonic diversity than ever before, each outfit also making their mark on the national scene to varying degrees.

The Hilltops — University of Mississippi graduate John Stirratt, his sister and Louisiana transplant Laurie Stirratt, and her husband Cary Hudson — were an original Americana outfit who toured extensively throughout the Southeast. John Stirratt later joined Wilco, after the Hilltops' demise in 1990. Sadly, the band only recorded a single album, *Big Black River*, before calling

it quits, but Laurie and John released *Arabella* in 2003, their first collaboration in a dozen years.

In the meantime, Laurie and Cary kept their collaboration intact, making Oxford, Mississippi, the launching point for a new band, Blue Mountain, soon after the Hilltops folded. With Cary on guitar, Laurie on bass, and drummer Matt Brennan (replaced by Frank Crouch in 1995), the group went on to release eight albums throughout their combined career. Five years after their 2002 breakup, the group reunited. By then, their reputation had grown, both in alt-country circles and among those who recognized them as one of Mississippi's foremost musical ambassadors.

The Windbreakers, a power-pop duo helmed by Tim Lee and Bobby Sutliff, were something of an anomaly. Their music had no direct link to the state's musical traditions, but their early series of albums and EPs established a penchant for riveting rock and roll with a determined edge and melodic under-tow. Today, Lee lives with his wife and musical collaborator Susan Bauer Lee in Knoxville, Tennessee, where they juggle two bands, the Tim Lee 3 and Bark. Nevertheless, their ties to their native state remain intact.

"The people that have come along and made great music have all been aware of their roots and tied into their roots, whether they were beholden to them or not," Lee observes. "They know the tradition because it's part of their DNA. The roots are there, but they're not making music that imitates them. There's a melding of cultures that you

"Mississippi is a conundrum
wrapped in an enigma.
It's this very mystery —
always held close to the
vest by its initiates — that
has created the legacy born
of the suffering known
as the blues."

Jimbo Mathus

don't necessarily get everywhere. It's a fertile breeding ground, no matter what kind of music there is. People think of Blue Mountain as this alt-country band, but there's every bit as much Robert Johnson in that music as there is Hank Williams. That's what makes it special."

Music is Everywhere

These days, Mississippi's musical diversity has become a defining element, as expressed through national touring acts like the Dickinsons' North Mississippi Allstars, Steve Forbert, Jimbo Mathus, John Murry, and the Weeks as well as lesser-known groups like Passing Parade, Dead Gaze, the Squirms, Swamp Babies, the Vibe Doctors, the Water Babies, the Neckbones, Ming Donkey, and Laurie Stirratt's new band, Teardrop City. These groups are pulling from Mississippi's deep roots to turn cities like Jackson, Oxford, and Hattiesburg into thriving centers of artistic activity once again. Hip-hop has become a vibrant part of the state's musical mix, too, with acts such as 5th Child, James Crow, Silas, and DJ Young Vernon contributing to the increasingly varied palette.

"I can't pinpoint a particular sound," Homework Town's Garrad Lee admits. "I work mainly with hip-hop artists, and that's huge here. Blues, of course, is still huge, especially electric blues. And I think we have a better indie scene than most people realize. We've put out albums from bands that I think are absolutely genius."

Many Mississippi artists agree that there is ample support these days for homegrown music and a growing number of venues where original music is played, even encouraged. Still, the situation isn't necessarily ideal. Mississippi's local musicians offer conflicting views.

Tim Lee remembers his childhood growing up in Jackson. "Back then," he says, "there really weren't bands that played original material exclusively. You had to play four sets of Beatles songs before you could play any of your own tunes. So it didn't take me long to start rebelling against that and trying to make other things happen. It's interesting to me how Jackson is today — there's a very fertile scene going on there. There's a

lot of support. There were people who liked live music 30 years ago, but they just wanted to dance to stuff they knew. Nowadays, the scene there is a lot more supportive, and there's a lot more interaction between the rock acts and the hip-hop acts. It's a really impressive thing to see."

"For a musician who knows the folk, blues, and country canon, and who isn't that concerned with money, playing opportunities are almost limitless," Jimbo Mathus says. "Then again, if I play 'Dixie' at the catfish house, hundred-dollar bills start flying!"

"Music is everywhere," Garrad Lee maintains. "Pretty much anywhere you go, someone is playing some kind of music. I book shows at Offbeat, a comic book/record store in Jackson, and at coffee shops, art studios, and venues like Hal and Mal's, Martin's, and Big Sleep's, to name a few. … On a Thursday night in Jackson you can hear a singer-songwriter at Hal and Mal's while you eat dinner, then go to the art museum and hear some hip-hop on the green space outside, and maybe later go to Martin's to see a national touring act, and end up at F. Jones Corner for late-night blues."

The Weeks' Sam Williams adds to this list of notable venues, citing Jackson's Duling Hall and Oxford's Proud Larry's. But, as many new venues as have popped up, making a living as a local musician in Mississippi is no easy task. Bobby Rush notes, "Where the cotton fields and clubs used to be … where there used to be 20 or more juke joints, the casinos put them out of business, leaving maybe two or three. But even the two or three are suffering because people are spending all of their money at the big casinos and leaving the mom-and-pop places high and dry. Many of the blues entertainers have to go out of state to continue to work because they can't find enough work in Mississippi. The people here didn't even embrace Elvis until he made it big."

"The state has come a long way in embracing its music as a tourist attraction," Mathus says. "Most of the time, I end up entertaining at picnics, political rallies, crawfish boils, and the like, [where I'm] in the same social stratum as the help. It's humbling but strangely freeing, being an entertainer and … [making music for] real people

doing real-life things and having music [as] a part of that very fabric of life. It's the Mississippi way."

A Mississippi Feel

These days, the Mississippi sound is hard to pin down. Some assert it's the blues, but, given the state's growing diversity and the fact that its music scene has been burgeoning in every direction for decades, no such generalization can suffice. "The main difference," Stirratt says, "is that it's got a gut-bucket, rootsy, dirty quality."

"I think there is a Mississippi feel more than a Mississippi sound," Williams of the Weeks suggests. "Something in the mud promotes this uninhibited raw expression that really doesn't come from anywhere else. There is a feeling in Mississippi music today that evokes the history of the blues and soul and country, but never feels contrived."

Ming Donkey sees it as something deeper. "It's starting to seem like a free-for-all again, at least from my experience," he muses. "People think there is a Mississippi sound, and plenty of people can make a buck off that theory. But if you're willing to walk into the dark, there are plenty of other audio experiences to be had that give general meaning to our tag as the birthplace of American music."

Garrad Lee agrees, and given the diversity of sounds that he works with, he's quick to recognize the bigger picture. "Mississippi is such a unique place," he says, "and there is a shared experience we all have from living here that I tend to hear flowing through the music. I think that is what ties it all together. … I think it's fair to say that most of the music is made by people who are just doing their thing. And I guess that's all any one of us in this state can do."

"There's such a long tradition of music, starting with the Delta blues," Tim Lee reflects. "You hear stories about guys coming down and working in the cotton fields and learning to play guitar from Junior Kimbrough and then it all kind of culminates with Elvis, this white guy who sounds black. The blues traditions and the country tradition and the folk tradition all kind of came together and it became a perfect melting pot. [Mississippi has] been fertile for a long time." ∎

Mississippi Blues Music Wall of Fame (Leland, Mississippi).

"It's the people that make a place great, and it's the people that have passed the tradition down, person to person, hand to hand." —Luther Dickinson

MADE IT THIS FAR

The many lives of Candi Staton
by Jonathan Bernstein

"When I'm in a conversation with anyone and it turns to music, I subconsciously hope they don't know about her. Then I get the pleasure of watching their face when they first hear 'Another Man's Woman' or 'Heart on a String.' That look of, 'Where has she been all my life?'"

John Paul White

WHEN SHE'S DRIVING AROUND — whether through the quiet streets near her home in Madison, Georgia, the rural back roads of surrounding Morgan County, or the sprawling interstate system that weaves through the Atlanta metro area, where all five of her children live — Candi Staton loves to listen to the radio. She has Sirius XM in her new BMW, and she can't get enough of it. "The First Lady of Southern Soul," as she's sometimes called, enjoys it all: hip-hop, gospel, classic rock, pop, even talk radio when she's in the mood.

When she's looking for a good story, Staton flips to the country station, drawn in by clever Music Row wordplay. "Oh, that's cute," she'll say to herself about whatever slick-titled song pops up in her display. When she wants to keep up with what's going on in the dance music world — in which Staton presides, to this day, as an influential trailblazer — she turns to the house music station, where, as she puts it, "all the songs are thousands of beats per minute." If she discovers a particularly catchy groove, she will crank the volume and bounce around in the driver's seat.

But if she's feeling more reflective, nostalgic, even, about her musical past, about the better part of a decade she spent touring the Chitlin' Circuit, performing the indelible R&B sides she recorded in Muscle Shoals during the late '60s and early '70s, Staton will switch to B.B. King's Bluesville station. There, she'll hear many of her contemporaries, most of whom she has, against all odds, outlived: men like King and Albert Taylor (both of whom she used to tour with), Muddy Waters, Bobby "Blue" Bland, and Ray Charles.

She once spent a week opening for Charles at the Aladdin Theatre in Las Vegas, in the fall of 1976. Charles was already an oldies act by then, but Staton was just starting her second life as a recording artist, having reinvented herself as a mainstream pop singer with her first Top 20 hit, "Young Hearts Run Free." Before each show, Staton would head over to Charles' dressing room, where the two sipped his drink of choice, amaretto and coffee, and shared wild stories about their past.

"Candi," Charles said during one of their pre-show hangouts, "you know, you're the female Ray Charles."

"What are you saying?" she replied.

"You're the female Ray Charles," he repeated. "You connect country and gospel and blues together. That's what I do."

"That was," says Staton, 40 years later, "one of the best compliments anyone could have ever given me."

Music in Multiple

Candi Staton has been drawing from these diverse strands of musical roots her whole life, whether as the teenaged lead singer of the Jewel Gospel Trio, who toured the country with Mahalia Jackson, Aretha Franklin, and the Soul Stirrers in the early '50s; or as the pioneering country-soul singer recording in Muscle Shoals; or as the disco-leaning pop star of the late '70s; or the devout gospel singer during the '80s and '90s; or as the newly emerged roots music veteran who has, over the past decade, embraced her multiple musical selves and sought to combine them all into something new.

The origins of Staton's sound can be traced back to the three types of AM radio stations — gospel, blues, and country — that her family could tune in when she was a child growing up in rural Hanceville, Alabama. "To me," says Staton, "it was all just music, and I loved all of it."

Though she has never earned the type of widespread acclaim that her contemporaries Aretha Franklin and Etta James received for their work in Muscle Shoals, the several dozen songs that she recorded at FAME Studios with producer Rick Hall between 1968 and 1974 endure today as some of the most vital pop recordings of the past 50 years.

"They define the New South to me," says Mark Nevers, a producer who has worked on several of Staton's most recent albums. "The feel of it, the Southernness of it, and knowing what she was singing about kind of sums up the hidden, overlooked thing that Muscle Shoals was."

These days, next-generation Alabama musicians like Jason Isbell, Dylan LeBlanc, John Paul White, Paul Janeway, and Browan Lollar all cite Staton as a primary influence. Outside of Alabama's

Americana revival, singers as different as Mary J. Blige, Shane MacGowan (lead singer of the Pogues), Sam Smith, Jessie J., Elton John, and Florence Welch have all professed their love for her music. Yet despite her influence, she is, as Lollar notes, still a "widely-held secret."

Why hasn't Staton, who was blending country, blues, jazz, gospel, rock, and pop — and, in so doing, was helping invent an entire genre of music called Americana, several decades before it had a name — received the type of late-career recognition that so many of her contemporaries have? Why did such fame elude her in the first place?

Ask Staton herself why she never became famous, and she'll give a straight-forward answer: "I really wanted it," she says, "but the guys that I chose to be in my life at the time were a big hindrance. Every time I got ready to go over that hump and get to another level, I would meet somebody that would not allow it. They would act crazy and stop my opportunities."

The more you learn about Staton's life, the more you learn her story of survival — specifically, the story of surviving violent cycles of abuse from men. After being molested by a family member at an early age, Staton has endured five failed marriages, most of which subjected her to physical abuse. Her third husband, a music promoter and serial abuser named Jimmy James, raped her, threatened her with a loaded gun, and once threatened her life by dangling her over a 24th story balcony. Such trauma brought Staton to the brink of suicide at a young age and resulted in a period of alcoholism in the late 1970s.

With all of that far in the rearview, Staton is at work on a new autobiography, *Young Hearts Run Free*, scheduled for release later this year, which she says will be a collection of "the stories behind the stories."

"I want other women to see that abuse is no joke," she says, "and you don't have to live in it. You can escape it. There are

red flags. That's the problem with domestic abuse: you say, 'Well, he didn't really mean it. Yeah, he slapped me; yeah, he gave me a black eye; yeah, he kicked me around, but it's okay now, we made it through.' But it's not. It's not okay. I had to learn that the hard way."

To understand the shortcomings and successes of Staton's career, then, is to appreciate the life of someone who has survived and overcome far more than any human should ever be expected to survive. As she puts it in a lovely blues ballad she'll soon be releasing: "It hasn't been easy … but I've made it this far."

Despite all she's endured, Staton remains busy well into her eighth decade. This summer, she's touring in Europe to celebrate the 40th anniversary of her biggest hit, the 1976 disco smash "Young Hearts Run Free." She is several times more popular in Europe, where she performs at large festivals and sold-out club dates, than she is here in the States. "The European mindset is so different from America," she says. "Here, you are as big as your latest hit. There, they go back into history, and you're like old wine, an antique, something precious, and they don't want to lose it. They don't want to hear the people who have learned from you; they want *you*."

But rather than rest on past accomplishments, Staton is still as stubbornly artistic as ever. When we spoke, she was just completing her forthcoming gospel record, *It's Time to Be Free*, and simultaneously putting the finishing touches on a separate dance/R&B album. She is frustrated by the lack of reception she's had for its debut single, "Shout out, Hallelujah," which merges two unlikely genres: gospel and disco-inspired house music. (She calls it "gospco.")

"I'm the kind of artist you can't keep up with," she says. "You don't put me in a box, because I'm going to find a way to get out. People try to put you in that traditional box, or this blues box, or this disco box, and I'm not going to do it. I'm going to sing exactly what's in my heart."

Top to bottom: Candi Staton in 1976; Staton with B.B. King and friends; Staton with John Paul White, Jason Isbell, and Rick Hall; Staton and Clarence Carter.

"**You don't put me in a box, because I'm going to find a way to get out. People try to put you in that traditional box, or this blues box, or this disco box, and I'm not going to do it. I'm going to sing exactly what's in my heart.**"

Candi Staton

Do Right Woman

The first person to ever tell Canzetta Maria Staton which type of music she was or wasn't allowed to sing was her mom. Rosie Sims approved of gospel, even country, laughing whenever her nine-year-old daughter ran around the house singing Nashville hits like Eddy Arnold's "Bouquet of Roses." The blues, on the other hand, were strictly forbidden. Yet, Staton's father, Earsie — an irresponsible, alcoholic dirt farmer with little patience for church — made sure his daughter learned about his favorite music whenever he could, sneaking her out to juke joints and playing blues on the radio when his wife wasn't around.

It wasn't until a young Staton and her family moved to Cleveland and started attending the Pentecostal Church of the Living God that she realized all the different types of music she loved could be combined. "They had the most unusual music that you ever heard in the church: a four-piece rhythm section, guitar, bass, drums, keyboards, even steel guitar," she says. "I was blown away because they had the type of music that you hear in clubs in the church."

Bishop Mattie Lou Jewell, an influential minister who ran a school in Nashville, took a liking to the Staton family in Cleveland, and convinced Canzetta and her sister Maggie to move to Nashville to attend the Jewell Academy and Seminary. Before long, the Staton sisters were touring the country as part of the Jewel Gospel Trio. Billboard described Canzetta's vocal on the group's 1957 single "Praying Time" by saying,

"Spirit is there with strong lead belting." Aretha Franklin, who saw the group perform, wrote in her autobiography that Canzetta's voice was "filled with feeling." The Jewel Gospel Trio toured the Philippines and the Bahamas, opened for Paul Robeson, and traveled the US with the era's greatest gospel acts.

Performing one evening at the Apollo Theater alongside the Staple Singers, Canzetta was stopped by a young Mavis Staples. "You know what," Mavis, four months Canzetta's junior, said to her as they walked up the steps to the Apollo. "I'm not going to try to call you by whatever your name is. I'll call you Candi, because you're sweet." The name stuck.

During her senior year of high school, Candi Staton, who had begun dating a preacher's son by the name of Joe Williams, became pregnant. "I thought of having an abortion but they weren't easy to get in 1959," she writes in her 1994 autobiography, *This Is My Story.* "I was miserable." Before she knew it, Staton was a mother of four and the wife of a jealous, controlling husband. "He literally kept me barefoot and pregnant for seven years," she wrote.

One evening, Staton's older brother snuck her out to a nightclub in Birmingham. She got on stage and sang an impromptu version of Aretha Franklin's recent hit, "Do Right Woman, Do Right Man," which ended up earning her a regular gig at the club. To no one's surprise, Joe Williams was no fan of Staton's new job, and the two divorced within months.

Staton soon recorded a few singles for some tiny local labels, including a catchy Motown-inspired tune called

"Now You've Got the Upper Hand" and a collaboration with country singer Billy Walker titled "The Judgement" (alternative title: "You Can't Judge a Man By the Color of His Skin"). Details on Staton's exact involvement on the latter remain hazy, but what is clear is that in 1968, the year Dr. Martin Luther King Jr. was killed and race riots broke out throughout the country, Staton released an anti-racist duet with a Grand Ole Opry stalwart born in 1929.

Just six weeks after her nightclub debut, Staton found herself opening for Clarence Carter, who would later become her second husband, and who, most importantly, would eventually introduce her to an enthusiastic, demanding record producer he had been working with in a small town in Northwest Alabama. That man's name was Rick Hall.

Singing It Out

A partial list of songs that Rick Hall and his legendary studio band, the Swampers, had recorded by the time Staton arrived in late 1968: "When a Man Loves a Woman," by Percy Sledge, "I'd Rather Go Blind" by Etta James, "Mustang Sally" by Wilson Pickett, "I Never Loved a Man (The Way I Love You)" by Aretha Franklin, "Sweet Soul Music" by Arthur Conley.

Staton's Muscle Shoals recordings sound and feel both integrally related to this well-recited Muscle Shoals canon and entirely apart from it. The FAME Studios mythology, so often characterized as a utopia of post-racial collaboration, is a story too irresistible

in its improbability: the tale of a dingy studio on the side of a dusty highway producing groundbreaking pop hit after groundbreaking pop hit during the half-decade between 1963 and 1968 (not exactly a shabby time in American pop music history in general).

But Staton's body of work at FAME — although she never had that career-defining smash hit, perhaps *because* she never did — sounds, nearly 50 years later, like a complete body of work. It's full of hardship survived, wisdom learned, pain transcended, and beauty imparted, with so much left to teach us. It's a collection of music that contains alternative understandings and secret histories of Muscle Shoals.

Though it ultimately eluded her, Staton came rather close to achieving mainstream superstardom. During her brief run at FAME, she enjoyed close to a dozen Top 10 R&B hits, with several songs crossing over to the pop charts. "Candi Staton could be the shooting star of soul," *Billboard* declared in 1971. That year, she was nominated for a Grammy for her rendition of Tammy Wynette's "Stand by Your Man" and again, just two years later, for one-upping Elvis with her soulful take on "In the Ghetto."

To get a proper sense of the power of Staton's extraordinary voice, consider, first, a singer without a name. "Unknown Female," is the credit, literally, on the 2011 compilation *The FAME Studios Story 1961–73.* The anonymous woman singing the cheating ballad "Another Man's Woman, Another Woman's Man" has a beautiful voice, delivering a perfectly lovely rendition of a song that surely would have sounded at home on the R&B charts in the late '60s.

When Staton sings "Another Man's Woman," the song becomes something else.

The way we feel
about each other baby
makes us do things
some folk just don't understand

She sings with gut-punch phrasing, pausing just long enough after "makes us do things" to linger in the fantasy a moment longer before she's interrupted by reality: "Some folk," she sings, her voice bending upward to a near-crack on the word "folk," as if she's a bit fearful, if not dismissive, of the man she knows she'll eventually go home to.

Staton inhabits the twin worlds of ecstasy and anguish, of love and abuse, carnal delight and physical torture during "Another Man's Woman," tossing them at each other until it becomes, in a way that's deeply unsettling, hard to tell which is which. "Turn my pleasure into pain," is how she puts it, much more eloquently, on "Heart on a String."

"Another Man's Woman" is a cheating song, a subject Staton always mastered with frightening ease. The subtext is plain enough: What, or who, is Staton running *from*?

Staton married Clarence Carter in 1970, the year "Another Man's Woman" was released. Her second husband ended up being as abusive as her first. When she threatened to leave Carter, after discovering he had been cheating on her, he assaulted her, leaving her "bruised from head to toe ... black eye, black arms," she wrote in her autobiography.

Although histories of Staton's music rarely, if ever, mention the awful physical abuses she faced at home during the period she was recording with Rick Hall, she has made it clear that, during that time, it was of course impossible to separate her dangerous personal life from her art.

"The tunes were always about women as victims," she said in 2004. "It was natural back then. The men were writing the songs. Women didn't have a voice.

"The men wrote songs that they wanted women to do: 'Please don't leave me baby,'" Staton says, mockingly, imitating the frequently regressive, occasionally demeaning lyrical depictions of femininity during those years, songs with titles like, "I'll Drop Everything and Come Running," "That's How Strong My Love Is," or "Stand by Your Man."

"You're begging with him, *pleading* with him. Look at the lyrics of 'For You': 'I'll do anything, just call my name and I'll come running for you. You can walk all over me, treat me any kind of way. If I'm sick in the bed and I knew you had a little cold, I would get up out of my bed and come sit by you.' Bull," Staton, not one to curse, says with a laugh. "You know a man had to write that, right? But those were the kinds of records male DJs would play. They loved to hear me beg."

"The reason I could actually do it," she continues, "Was because I was in relationships at that time that were abusive. I felt the emotion of being in that predicament. It was almost like therapy, and now I had a platform. I have somebody who's going to listen to me."

Pause for a moment to contemplate Staton's statement. Consider its radicalism, the way it suggests that there are two ways to hear her sing a song like "I'm Just a Prisoner (Of Your Good Lovin')." One way is to hear Candi Staton, "the new American singing star," as a 1970 ad boasted, singing about a relationship that's subsumed her with its sensual force. Another is to hear a woman, fearful for her very life, crying for help.

Consider, then, what Staton does with songs like "Someone You Use" and "Heart on a String," transforming lyrics she's been handed — stories of housewife complacency, intoxicating love, and irresistible submission — into worlds of tragedy, comedy, lust, betrayal, trauma, intoxication, strength, and survival.

Consider 1971's "Too Hurt to Cry" as not simply the tale of a heartbroken lover grieving over an ex but of a woman, numbed by trauma, who slowly begins to reclaim her own sense of self through the process of vocalizing her devastation. "I neglected myself, baby, devoted my life to you," Staton sings in a soft blues lament. Lines later, she's shouting: "I feel so bad, I could just die." She delivers those words with a glee so triumphant you may forget what she's actually saying. Finally, she's telling us, I can feel again.

Inferring an artist's personal life in their music is, more often than not, a misguided fool's errand, but hearing Staton discuss the way her early music with FAME served as a form of therapy — her *only* real way of discussing her personal problems at the time — it becomes difficult, if not impossible, to hear her music without a newfound sense and deep appreciation of the music's layers of traumatic pain and deep tragedy.

With no one to confide in or seek support from, Staton sought refuge in her music. There, paradoxically — and in a way, tragically — she found herself singing about situations that shared uncanny similarities with the dangerous mistreatment she was subjected to at home. If she suspected her husband of cheating on her (a frequent occurrence), she says, "I can't talk to him about it because if I do, it'll end up in a fight. So I can sing it out."

A New Generation

For young Alabama musicians growing up in the decades after the height of Muscle Shoals' musical renaissance, Staton's music often became a touchstone at an early age. For these artists, many of whom make up the core of the resurgence of roots music in the Shoals region, hearing Staton was a transformative experience.

Paul Janeway, who calls Staton's debut *I'm Just a Prisoner* "one of the quintessential Muscle Shoals records," says it was the "grit" and the "urgency" of Staton's voice that caught him. For Dylan LeBlanc, it was the "depth," the "sadness and loss," in her voice that profoundly influenced his own vocal approach. For John Paul White, it was her "conviction and purpose." "I believe every word she sings," White says. "She breaks my heart, and picks me up. I feel her loss, and she gives me hope."

For Browan Lollar, Janeway's bandmate in St. Paul and the Broken Bones, it was more of a sense that he was finally hearing the original source of so much of the music he loved. "Candi's a prime example of the type of artist where, if you like the way this record that came out in 1999 sounded, and then you find the record that influenced that record, and then you go find the record that influenced *that* record, and you go back and back, eventually you wind up at Candi Staton."

"There's a raspiness and almost a bit of a yodel in Candi's voice that really attracts me," says Jason Isbell. "It breaks from one note to the next, sometimes really sharply. It's something that Otis Redding had, and it's something that Sam Moore had, that I think sets those singers apart, because you don't have to use a lot of vocal acrobatics to get your point across. It winds up being very soulful and tender, but it's not overwrought and there isn't too much obvious effort. That's the hardest trick to pull off."

"More people should have her music in their lives," says White. That being said, he takes great enjoyment in introducing others to Staton's music. "When I'm in a conversation with anyone and it turns to music, I subconsciously hope they don't know about her. Then I get the pleasure of watching their face when they first hear 'Another Man's Woman' or 'Heart on a String.' That look of, 'Where has she been all my life?'"

Hundreds of thousands of people must have had that very look on their face when, in 2004, Honest Jon's, a small record store in London, partnered with EMI and released the first-ever comprehensive compilation of Staton's Muscle Shoals recordings. "There's a pantheon of soul singers, and Candi has an undisputed place there," says Mark Ainley, the owner of Honest Jon's. "When EMI started asking us to look for material to reissue, Candi was the very first thing we thought of, and it was by far the most successful thing that we put out."

Crowds in Europe "thought I only did 'Young Hearts Run Free' and 'You Got the Love,' songs like that," says Staton, who credits the compilation as a large reason why she is such a superstar in Europe today. "They never dreamed I was a blues singer."

With a renewed interest in her R&B roots, at age 66 Candi Staton made her formal return to secular music after spending over 20 years exclusively singing gospel. The resulting record,

2006's *His Hands*, is an openhearted reflection on her past struggles and righteous survival. With its moving title track written by indie songwriter Will Oldham, it was also Staton's first collaboration with a younger generation of roots musicians who view Staton as musical royalty.

"She didn't want to repeat what she had already done," says Mark Nevers, the producer of *His Hands*. "She was not 20 years old anymore, and she wasn't going to sing any more songs about being your baby."

When Staton met up with Nevers, she refused to sing some of the darker material the young producer had set aside for her. "If you start singing about those things," she told him, "they'll start happening to you." Staton had already been there. During the days of her debut single, "I'm Just a Prisoner," she says she really did "feel like a prisoner," as though some part of her had willed her misfortune into being through her music. Staton was determined to go a different way this time. Isbell, who has gotten to know her well over the years, says, "She goes to a lot of lengths to make sure that her life stays positive."

His Hands ended up being her first real opportunity to explore her deep roots in country music, with covers by Merle Haggard and Charlie Rich. "Her whole thing was that she never got to make a record with heavy country influences," says Nevers. "At first, some people were like, 'This isn't a Candi Staton record,' but it was the record she wanted to make."

What I've Always Done

Staton reunited with Rick Hall for several songs on her 2014 album *Life Happens*, which included the highlight "I Ain't Easy to Love," a duet featuring John Paul White and Jason Isbell. The recording of that song was featured in the 2013 documentary *Muscle Shoals*.

Yet even with the renewed interest in the musical history of Muscle Shoals (brought about, in large part, from the documentary), Staton's own R&B legacy has remained in the shadows. Not a single word is uttered in the film regarding Staton's own FAME recordings. Instead, the scene where she records "I Ain't Easy to Love" is utilized exclusively to emphasize Hall's tireless work ethic.

While Staton has been tangentially involved with the resurgence in Muscle Shoals music, participating in the occasional one-off tribute concert, she has yet to see the type of celebratory critical reappraisal that the Shoals studio band, the Swampers, and Hall have enjoyed from the film. Still, her influence continues to extend in unexpected ways beyond her circle of influence in the region.

Her 1986 European hit "You Got the Love" became an alt-rock charting hit in the States for Florence & the Machine in 2009. A few years later, after recording *Life Happens*, Staton teamed up with one of her many admirers, East Nashville singer-songwriter Caitlin Rose. The two wrote and recorded a duet in Muscle Shoals that was never released.

"She wasn't just singing these love songs; it was more about having something to say, like early day Beyoncé. With Aretha and Etta James, there was definitely a message and it was really a resurgence for female singers,'" says Leigh Watson, who alongside her sister Chandra makes up the country-folk duo the Watson Twins. Like Staton, Leigh grew up singing in church with her sister. "Whereas a lot of singers are emulating other singers in order to find their voice," Leigh says, "Candi had a voice that was her own and was personal to her. As singers, that's what we look for."

Indeed, Staton continues to inspire artists across genres and generations, including her longtime friend Ann McCrary, a Nashville gospel singer who has enjoyed newfound popularity in the

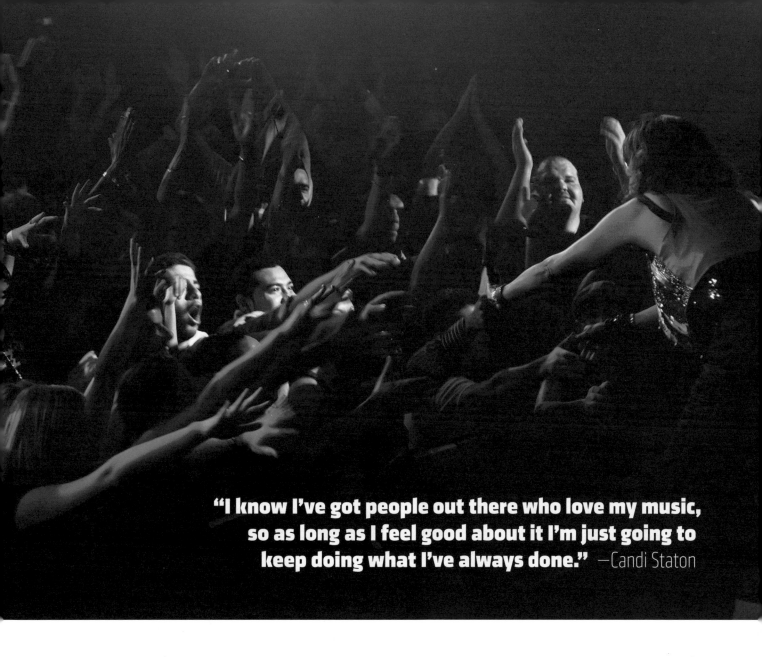

"I know I've got people out there who love my music, so as long as I feel good about it I'm just going to keep doing what I've always done." —Candi Staton

Americana community in recent years with her group the McCrary Sisters.

"You can turn the radio on, and I don't care if she's singing gospel or not, with Candi Staton you always know who you were listening to. Those are things that influence me," says McCrary. "[She] told me: 'Be yourself. The gift that you have, God gave it to you, so develop it and don't try to sound like anybody else.'"

Staton, for her part, has followed her own advice, and she's unburdened, nowadays, by expectations others have about what her music is supposed to sound like. "I know I've got people out there who love my music, so as long as I feel good about it I'm just going to keep doing what I've always done," she says.

"I'm going to sing a little country, I'm going to sing a little blues, and I'm going to sing a little gospel."

As an unlikely progenitor of American roots music, Staton represents the best impulses of the genre. Her vision of the music is inclusive and without borders; it has just as much room for the intricate rhythms of dance music and the life-affirming joy of born-again gospel as it does for traditionally revered roots genres like blues, folk, and country.

After divorcing her fifth husband in 2012, Staton, 76, is relieved, finally, that her tumultuous, troubled days seem to be behind her. "I've been through the storms and I'm in a good place now," she says. "I've got grown children and

grandkids around. I've got a lot of love around me."

In the last decade, Staton has started revisiting her earliest material more often, and now and then she'll find herself putting on one of her FAME records.

"I listen to those records Rick and I did together, and I go back," she says. "I thank God that I'm not there anymore — that was a period of my life and that chapter's closed, and that I know I won't repeat it. But it's great to reminisce and to thank God that I came through it unscathed, you know?

"I don't have any scars," she adds. "I don't have anything that I have not gotten over. I just go on and say, 'Oh well, that was that,' and I'm done." ∎

MOVING HOUSE

**These days,
Elizabeth Cook
is musically
unsupervised**

by Allison Moorer

"I have the disease to please, and of course I wanted to please my parents. That stays with you. When they passed it was like being home alone. I've become musically unsupervised."

Elizabeth Cook

IT'S IMPOSSIBLE NOT TO NOTICE Elizabeth Cook. I did, the first time I saw her at Nashville's Exit/In one Tuesday night, at Billy Block's Western Beat Barn Dance, during the late 1990s. She had just started to emerge on the Nashville singer-songwriter scene. She was blond, beautiful, seemingly a little on the shy side, sporting cat-eye glasses, and wielding a voice that made my ears perk up and my heart swell all at the same time. It was obvious that she was a serious talent, though there was an air about her that suggested something else running beneath the surface, something beyond her voice and beauty.

We got to know each other slowly but surely. We saw each other at parties and gatherings and commiserated about the degradation of auditioning for this record label or that publisher around town. We moaned and complained, but never dwelled on it. We knew it was only part of the game we'd signed up to play, and hopefully win.

As Elizabeth and I grew to be friends, I found out she wasn't shy at all, and what I'd intuited beneath the surface turned out to be a big brain and a deep soul. She was an Artist, with a capital A.

Elizabeth has since carved out a career for herself that is not only successful by anyone's measuring stick, but enviable as well. She's racked up over 400 appearances on the Grand Ole Opry to date (she quit counting after her daddy died). She hosts a beloved program on Sirius XM's Outlaw Country channel called *Apron Strings* and is a certifiable radio star, as much as anyone can be these days. She's played hundreds of shows, written plenty of songs, and made well-received albums. She's never made a note of music she couldn't stand by, and has been authentic every step of the way. But it's been six years since *Welder*, her last bold and brave full-length album, and four since *Gospel Plow*, an EP inspired by the church of her childhood.

A lot has happened since those days. One of the things I've learned in the years since I first met Elizabeth is this: If you're an Artist with a capital A, you're going to be paying attention. And if you're paying attention, you're going to change. I'll leave the math on that up to y'all. But I will tell you she has a new record in the can called *Exodus of Venus* (released June 17 on Agent Love Records/Thirty Tigers). And once again, it's impossible not to notice Elizabeth Cook.

She and I caught up over FaceTime this spring. She was at her home in Nashville, and I was at mine in New York City.

ELIZABETH COOK: Look at what I woke up to this morning. I don't know if you can see it, but it snowed cherry blossoms. [She's out in her yard.]

ALISON MOORER: That's gorgeous. … I want to talk to you about this new record and a couple other things.

So. *Exodus of Venus.* I've listened to it over and over, and it's just super deep sounding and big, and deeply groovy. It's the biggest piece of music I've heard from you. … It's rockier and more atmospheric. It's lyrically deep and insightful. I hear you cutting loose, I hear you asking questions, I hear you accepting yourself and the world, I hear you being brave.

EC: [Laughs.] Yeah, I blew my shit up, you know. It's taken balls to do it. And I still don't know what I'm doing. I'm feeling pretty, you know, freaked out, but better. [I have] more solid footing all the time. And making this record and putting it out is part of that process, as you know.

AM: Well, tell me, if you want to … about the blowing up. I know what blowing up feels like. I've done it myself.

EC: I bet you do! You know, I had the good fortune for a long time in my life of being shielded from tragedy, unlike so many folks. And then all of a sudden, over about a two-year period, my daddy died, my mother-in-law died, my father-in-law died, my brother-in-law died, my brother died, the farm burned down, my sister got a divorce, and then I got a divorce. All of that happened in a really short amount of time. So it seemed like every six weeks I was nursing somebody on their deathbed, or going to a funeral, or in divorce court. And those are dark places to reside in for that long a time.

AM: Well, you know I always say that sometimes life changes things for you, whether or not you're conscious of anything needing changing. Sometimes the universe just takes over. It's pretty painful to change, and it takes a lot of strength to get through it. I hear a lot of strength and fighting back on *Exodus of Venus*, and that's so exciting to me because the greatest art is personal. That's why we make it. It's our way of coping, but it's also our way of reaching out to other people and saying "you're not alone."

EC: Yeah! It's our job. That is the assignment.

AM: The record just sounds beautiful, the songs are great, this sounds to me like a country-rock outlaw record.

EC: Dexter Green [producer] had a ton to do with that. I don't know how to make those sounds and do that with guitar and write riffs and stuff, so … It allowed me to focus on other things to not have to do that part.

AM: The worrying about the producing part?

EC: Yeah. … I co-wrote most of the record with Dexter, and it was the process of him playing me some deep, dark groove on the guitar that I would just start singing over, and it would speak to me, and it would have this really cool sound, and I would start saying something over it and then dig in the journals for the lyrics. It was so easy — and rewarding. I had never heard my music sound like that before. I was just really enjoying it. I'm enjoying playing the music live a lot.

AM: Let's talk about Dexter a minute. How did you meet him and what makes you click?

EC: Yeah, what makes us click? I mean, chemistry! I was not gonna do this, you know. I had plenty of things to get together and focus on and coupling up again was not something that made a lot of sense on paper. But again, it was one of those things that just happened. There's a line in "Exodus of Venus": "Far-away lands suffered a plague the minute you put your hand on my leg."

AM: I heard that and said, "Uh huh. Been there."

EC: Sexy talk! I'd known him for a long time. Jason Isbell and I had recorded at his house, so he had helped me record things there in the neighborhood when I just needed something done quickly, but I really didn't know what he did. He's kind of a quiet guy. I knew he had a studio and was nice and cute and he would help me sometimes. One night he gave me a ride home from the bar and …

AM: Oh hell.

EC: Yeah. I was like "Damn it!" I was changing management, breaking that bond. … I lost everyone around me. Friends fell away, the industry fell away, things got thin. It's been thin! And that was right when we got together. That chapter of chaos was about to start.

AM: I always say be careful who you make music with, you might end up moving house.

EC: [Laughs.] Amen.

AM: Singing and making music with people is such a visceral experience that you can't help but connect. And when there's a spark there anyway, watch out. Tell me where you recorded this record.

EC: We made it at Sound Emporium [in Nashville]. We had a wonderful week in there with great players. …

AM: I know. Willie Weeks, Buddy Miller, Matt Chamberlain, Patty Loveless … this is a great cast.

EC: Ridiculous.

AM: Getting in the studio and making stuff up is just so much fun.

EC: Yeah. And I knew that. I knew that when all the rehab stuff went down I was like, this is not it.

AM: Do you want to talk about that? … I remember worrying about you and sending you a note saying such after seeing you at the Americana Music Awards in 2014, when all the rumors started flying around. I thought, "What?"

EC: Oh right. You've known me too long.

AM: Right. Folks might be surprised to hear this but you and I are sorority sisters. We are both Kappa Deltas! We don't drink in our letters or smoke standing up. I just didn't think what I was hearing was the whole story.

EC: Right. I had definitely gotten too skinny. It was from stress — it wasn't from dieting.

AM: Well, death will do that to you.

EC: Yes. And divorce! I called it the Divorce and Death Diet. Then there were medications and drugs that I was partaking in to cope, but I wasn't directly addicted to any one thing. I was just medicating randomly with different stuff, and I made some bad choices.

That day in particular I [accidentally] took a toxic mix of pills. But I was still fine. I went and did all my gigs. I did everything I was supposed to do that day, I didn't understand. But the people who were around me that had fallen away, that then all of sudden were in town and saw me for the first time in six months, cancelled my tour, [which was supposed to be] my nut for the rest of the year. They didn't want me getting on a tour bus with Todd Snider for a month. They thought that maybe I was anorexic, or bulimic — they just didn't know.

They all teamed up and presented the rehab idea as a vacation and said, "If something's wrong then we'll get to the bottom of it, and if not you'll get a vacation."

Oh my God, that was traumatizing. I was institutionalized and I don't do well with that. It wasn't for me. But it serves a purpose and I learned a lot, and I look back now and I think it was probably supposed to happen.

AM: That particular thing has saved God knows how many lives, but you might've just needed a break.

EC: It was a fake spa. When I got in there, they weighed me in the dark, they wouldn't tell me if I was gaining or losing. [They put me on] a very regimented diet and I was starving all the time. My appetite was coming back. They thought I was purging because even with the protein shakes, etc., I wasn't gaining weight fast enough according to their science. I got in trouble for wearing my sunglasses inside because I had a migraine — shit like that. And I just didn't do well with it. But we [ruled] some things out that weren't wrong, so that was good. I learned a lot and moved on.

AM: That particular thing — dealing with our bodies as women, who are looked at a lot — has always been a struggle for me. When I saw you that night I thought you looked thin, but I've been too thin before and it doesn't scare me as much as it does other people. I've been accused of having an eating disorder, too. It's a difficult thing to be picked apart so much. Now we're getting older. There comes a time when you think, "This is who I am, this is what I look like, I'm going to try to look the best I can but I'm not going to expect to look like I did when I was 25 anymore, nor should anyone else expect that of me."

EC: Right. Absolutely. I mean when you're bred to believe that your appearance is part of your value ...

AM: We could talk for days about that.

EC: Add in being an entertainer. Then try and have integrity as an artist. And balance how good-looking you can be. There's a lot of conflicting information there. I'm fortunate to have strong sisters and beautiful people in my family, and I've just come to peace with a lot of things.

I'm supposed to — and women, I believe, are supposed to — pass into a different way of looking and feeling and feminine energy [as we age]. It just shifts. I'm okay with that.

I enjoy feeling sexual. I'm not one to believe that we should sacrifice our sexual power and femininity in the name of feminism. I believe it's biological and it's part of a power that there is nothing wrong with embracing and having fun with. I enjoy it when I feel like I look good. So I'm going to keep putting effort into it, I guess.

[Now, for me, feeling good is] more and more about energy, spirit, and presence, instead of just the aesthetics. It's just shifting. I feel like what we as women have to offer shifts as we get older. It goes from the physical to the metaphysical. That's natural and can be awesome.

AM: It becomes more about your insides showing up on your outside. And once you get comfortable in your skin, it's way easier to let that happen.

I want to talk to you about how losing your parents affected your artistry. You know I lost mine, too, so something that has always been a theme in my life is dreaming their dreams, saying their sayings, living my life, in a way, for them, [and] carrying out their wishes because they aren't here to do it. I know you were very close to your parents and they were musical, and were supportive of your musical dreams, but I think also probably pushed you to do it. Correct me if I'm wrong.

EC: Well, it was an earnest thing that came from love and excitement and pride. But yes. And they didn't realize it. And that's something I've learned in therapy. They loved me and that was genuine, and they thought they were doing great and were just so proud. But I was being used.

AM: I'll never forget hearing, "Mama you wanted to be a singer, too."

EC: Oh, wow. That's an old one. But, yeah. I totally did it for them. Right before Mama died, I had just started writing for the *Welder* album, 2008, and I had written "El Camino," and I played it for Mama in my car, driving her to the grocery store, and her response was, "Elizabeth, really."

EC: Do you feel like not having them around has freed you? Would you have made *Exodus of Venus*, if they were still alive?

EC: No. They were more and more confused about my career because they didn't understand — to them you're either Reba McEntire or the local lounge singer, with no in-between. It was hard for them to understand how that [in-between] could exist, and that's where I've existed.

[At the end,] they started to find peace with that, so I think I was freeing up somewhat anyway because they had to start letting go of the idea that I wasn't going to be Reba McEntire.

But "Heroin Addict Sister?" I don't know if I would've written that while my mother was alive. It was so important to her that her children get along. I didn't plan it, I didn't wait on purpose. I just realized that I probably would not have naturally gone there. I have the disease to please, and of course I wanted to please my parents. That stays with you. When they passed it was like being home alone. I've become musically unsupervised.

AM: I always say when you're an orphan you've got no one to answer to and nowhere to go for Christmas. ... It's a tradeoff. There is a freedom that comes with losing your folks. It's a sad freedom, but it is still freedom. You feel loosened from those expectations. You also don't get the approval that you crave so much.

EC: That's right. That's right.

AM: Let's talk about "Tabitha Tuders' Mama." I lost it when I heard that one. I have a little boy and I can't stand the thought of losing him, as no parent can. When I first listened to the song, I wondered how you did it, but then I decided that you don't have to be a mama to feel empathy for one. Tell me what inspired you to write it.

EC: I think that I saw some parallels between this working class, blue-collar, lower economic class family and my family.

This was my mother's greatest fear, that I would get snatched. I almost did. When I was 11, a guy tried to pick me up in his car. When I realized that he was creepy, I turned around and ran, but he went for me. I ran, and he took off. I think about — had he succeeded — the situation my family would've found themselves in.

I believe there's a stigma attached to the economics of the situation. Why does it feel like it's more tragic to lose a rich little girl than a poor one? And I [wonder], "Are black children not abducted?" Cause I don't ever see anything about that. So there's almost a value assigned, and we were a poor family. ... What if the town would've thought, because we were trashy or whatever they thought about us, that there was some shenanigan that trashy people partake in or I had run off with some older man or something.

I look at pictures of this little girl [Tabitha Tuders, a 13-year-old who was abducted in Nashville in 2003], I've got them right here, it's like ... She's holding an alligator. ... I don't know, she's a little girl. And I just felt like there was an injustice in the stigma attached to it because [of the] economics.

When you go down that street now, with all that's happening with real estate in East Nashville, the big condo things are on both sides of their house. The pressure they must be under — how many developers want to knock their house down? But that's her home. And what if she tries to come home?

AM: Yeah. That's pretty profound. But you've never shied away from commentary. You do it with "Evacuation" and "Methadone Blues" on this album, and you've done it with earlier songs. I so appreciate it because it's so hard to do successfully and without being preachy. You do it very well.

All right sister, well best of luck and love with it all. It's been so good to talk to you today. The record is amazing and I'm so proud of you.

EC: I wanna know how you're doing!

AM: I'll turn off the tape recorder. ■

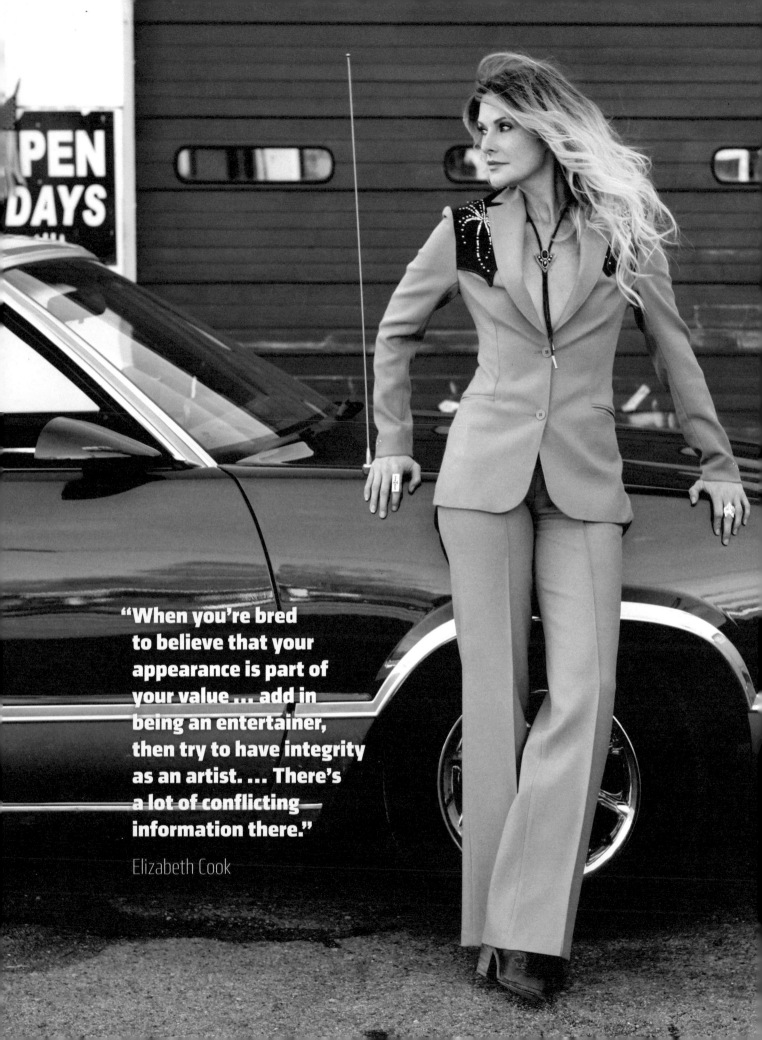

"When you're bred to believe that your appearance is part of your value ... add in being an entertainer, then try to have integrity as an artist. ... There's a lot of conflicting information there."

Elizabeth Cook

Schonbeck's Intriguing Instrumentarium

PHOTOGRAPHS COURTESY OF
THE MASSACHUSETTS MUSEUM
OF CONTEMPORARY ART

Over a half-century, Gunnar Schonbeck built an arsenal of musical instruments. Among them: a nine-foot banjo, drums made from aircraft nose cones, an eight-foot-tall marimba, welded-steel harps, countless steel drums, zithers, pan pipes, tubular chimes, and triangular cellos. This bizarre instrumentarium was tucked away in an attic at Bennington College in Vermont, where Schonbeck taught, composed, and made music for over 40 years. His philosophy was that "everything has its sound and you just have to bring it out." He did this not only through his inventions, but also through interactive community concerts in which he invited students, friends, and neighbors to participate in ad hoc ensemble concerts. At the peak of his career, he had more than 1,000 handmade instruments in his collection.

Schonbeck died in 2005, and this collection of his instruments was brought to MASS MoCA in 2011. It will be on display when the museum opens its next phase, in spring 2017.

opposite:

Glenn Kotche plays Schonbeck's nine-foot banjo in MASS MoCA galleries during Wilco's Solid Sound Festival.

Close-up of an oversized instrument
based on a Chinese guzheng.

Schonbeck made several different sizes of these one-string cellos, designed so that a person with no musical skills can play them. When played in a group, they automatically create a chord.

opposite:

**Schonbeck carved a whimsical face
on the front of this oversized guitar.**

this page and opposite:

A collection of several Schonbeck-

WITH (AND AGAINST) THE GRAIN

Guitars by Mario Desio.

Luthiers build sound and community by breaking the mold *by Deborah Crooks*

ON A TYPICAL DAY IN HIS MISSION District live/work studio, Peter Whitehead reaches for one of the dozens of lutes, lyres, fiddles, and "canjos" he's made to start the long work of writing music. Meanwhile, across the San Francisco Bay, luthier Mario Desio cuts the soundboard for a new guitar he's building in his East Bay home and workshop. While Desio and Whitehead create vastly different instruments — for very different musicians — they're each motivated by a wide-ranging curiosity about sound and a penchant for handmade, homemade things. And, in the process of building instruments, the two have helped forge, inspire, and strengthen their local music communities.

Both of these men came to California from elsewhere. Whitehead arrived from England in 1981. Since then, he has assembled a dynamic career at the confluence of instrument building, composing, visual arts, choreography, and performance. When he isn't composing music for renowned choreographers like Mikhail Baryshnikov, scoring for film, and building his handmade instruments, Whitehead might be singing Leonard Cohen songs with the 30-member men's a cappella group Conspiracy of Beards, readying a short solo set for an art

Homemade instruments by Peter Whitehead.

opening, or improvising with his instrumental folk-jazz trio, Closer to Carbon.

Desio, meanwhile, moved from New York in 1977 to pursue music, and has, for the past six years, built guitars for a diverse who's who of Bay Area songwriters: country-noir crooner Maurice Tani (77 El Deora), folk-rock strummer Jeff Pehrson (Box Set, Further), brainy troubadour Ira Marlowe, and noted lead guitarist Shelley Doty among them. Also, like Whitehead, he is in constant communication with his musically minded peers. He takes a break from sanding and shaping wood in his workshop to have lunch with fellow musicians like Tani and Grammy-winning electronic music innovator Roger Linn (most famous for inventing the LM-1 Drum Computer). He posts photo albums of works in progress on Facebook and plans gatherings for people whose guitars he built.

'I Got Into Sound'

Before he started building instruments, Desio spent many years immersed in the San Francisco music scene, penning acoustic folk songs and playing in a wide range of projects, from the bands he fronts — Mario Speedwagon and the Secret Identities — to theater and hardcore rock bands. All the while, he worked as a contractor to pay the bills. He met many of his current clients early in their careers, when he and they were playing at bustling songwriter nights at San Francisco's Owl and Monkey and Bazaar cafés or at the Freight & Salvage in Berkeley.

"I got into sound," says Desio during a recent interview, describing his lifelong love affair with the guitar. It began when he was a youth listening to the Beatles and followed him to the West Coast unabated.

"All the different sounds," he exclaims. "I wanted more sounds to play with. I loved my first Martin D-35. That was a great guitar. As time went by, I realized Gibsons have a great sound. So I went and bought a Gibson. ... Then I started going crazy. I got a Strat, then I got *a better* Strat. Then I thought I had to have a Gretsch because they have unique pickups."

By the early aughts, Desio was a new father, and his house was filled with nearly 30 instruments. That's when his wife put her foot down. "After 28–29 guitars, she said, 'That's enough, no more guitars!'" Desio laughs. "Our house was small and it was getting expensive."

Shortly before he exceeded his home's carrying capacity for instruments, Desio took his Gibson to respected luthier Alan Perlman for a fret job and a new bridge. "He fixed it, and I mentioned I'd like to build a guitar," Desio remembers. "He said, 'You understand wood, you can do it.' And I realized this is my loophole: I can't *buy* any more guitars, but I can make them."

Still, Desio's entry into luthiery was riddled with fits and starts. He started building a Django Maccaferri copy. Reaching an impasse, he abandoned it to try building two flat-top guitars. But he put them all aside when he heard that his old friend, Los Angeles-based folk-pop songwriter David Grossman, had his Gibson Hummingbird stolen.

"All my memories of him are with that guitar," Desio recounts. "So I put everything on hold and built him a replacement. I started it in January 2011, and finished it by [the] end of March."

It was the first acoustic guitar he completed. Buoyed by the instrument's reception and the accompanying interest from his Bay Area songwriting community, Desio began taking commissions from more of his musical friends and building in earnest.

In the years since, he has made a practice of using reclaimed or repurposed materials for many of his guitars. His ever-developing curiosity about the sounds and tones different woods yield led him to experiment with materials outside the mahogany, maple, and Brazilian rosewood trinity that many luthiers consider ideal for their craft. These days, Desio's shop is filled with pieces of walnut and cocobolo, Indian rosewood, reclaimed redwood, and remnants of vintage spruce pianos.

Tani, San Francisco songwriter and bandleader Pam Brandon (of Belle Monroe and Her Brewgrass Boys), and Berkeley musician and podcaster Vanessa Lowe all have Desio guitars with soundboards made from recycled piano (the fret dots of Brandon's parlor guitar are made from old ivory piano keys), hinting at an emerging signature of their builder.

"I'm chasing something," Desio admits. "I've read that [piano top] is not going to be any better, [because] you end up with a four-piece top, which [supposedly] isn't right ... the glue can come unglued. ... But the glue is Hyde glue and it held the piano together for 100 years, so it's not going to fall apart." More important than whatever Desio is chasing, the people who own his guitars are pleased. "I don't really know if it makes a difference," notes Tani, whose guitar's top comes from a 100-year-old upright piano. "But I figure a billion notes have already been played through it, so it's got to sound good."

Finding the Music

Growing up in England, Whitehead's early inspiration also included the Beatles. Like Desio, his first instrument was a guitar, but he was also deeply influenced by Brian Eno, Robert Wyatt, and Frank Zappa. As an adult, his extensive travels throughout Southeast Asia further expanded his ear.

During a lengthy trip to Vietnam, when he had nothing to play, Whitehead constructed his own instrument, based on a traditional East Asian folk instrument. "I loved the rebabs, [which are] basically a two-stringed fiddle," he says. "I loved those in Indonesia and in Mongolia ... in the Middle East. Two-stringed instruments are all over the Arab world."

He wanted to capture that sound, but he was wary about appropriating the culture. "I thought if I make my own version, with my own particular style, I could find my own music," he says. "I basically copied the form of [the rebab], but used my own materials. I didn't know how to play it, so I had to learn how to play it."

When he returned to the States, Whitehead began building more instruments, everything from "canjos" (banjos built from baking tins) to harps made from eucalyptus tree branches and wooden spoons. But he wasn't interested in building instruments simply for the sake of making a weird or far-out object. He was chasing the best sounds.

Whitehead met other instrument builders, including Oliver DiCicco, with whom he cofounded the Mobius

> ## "I realized this is my loophole: I can't buy any more guitars, but I can make them."
>
> Mario Desio

Operandi ensemble, which composed and performed music on all-original, homemade instruments. He contributed to Beth Custer's Vinculum Symphony, which combined chamber musicians and experimental instrument builders. And he connected with the thriving San Francisco modern dance community, scoring numerous pieces and collaborating on live performances.

At a spring appearance in a San Francisco art gallery, Whitehead peformed two differently textured arrangements of the same song, choosing instruments from a selection containing one of his first versions of the rebab, whose body utilized the wooden part of an ice bucket. He also had a balloon flute fashioned from a bit of pipe, a loop pedal, and a Yamaha FG180 guitar.

"The instruments I'm really focusing on now have to do with harmonics," he says, "and they're all really simple. The flute — there are no finger holes. One has a ball in it that slides up and down to change the pitch. The fiddle only has two strings and no frets. But I play conventional instruments as well, and I like using electronics."

Community of Creation

For both Desio and Whitehead, going with and against the grain has resulted in their work rippling through and beyond their own communities. At the same time Desio is mulling placing a few of his guitars in local venues to be used as house instruments, he has a patent pending on a new structural design for guitars. A few months ago, Whitehead was preparing to fill a gallery with a smorgasbord of his instruments and lead a musical mini-marathon performance as part of the 2016 San Francisco International Arts Festival. "[My plan is] to have a roomful of instruments and work my way through them," he says. "Guitars as well as weird acoustic things, electronic fiddles and flutes, and then maybe I'll use loops.

"I'm interested in [an instrument] becoming an access [point] to a language, to expression, to finding a voice," he continues. "One of my favorite things is being in a studio on a weekday, with dancers, making something. ... Dancers exist in this very physical world and music is invisible, intangible. They too get inspired by sound. You can see it. It changes what they're doing."

Desio has begun to host semi-regular showcases of his work, called "A Night of Desio Guitars," often at the Bazaar Café or the Monkey House, Marlowe's Berkeley listening room. Like the glue he uses, his guitars have served as a community reinforcement for the musicians who came up in the San Francisco Bay Area, many of whom are now too busy playing their respective shows to see each other play often. On one such evening, a dozen acoustic guitars — a baritone, a koa J-45, a semi-baritone, a sunburst dreadnought, a parlor — are waiting to be utilized by their fingerstyle-playing, Grateful Dead-interpreting, funk-grooving, and bluegrass-picking owners. The instruments make an impressive display against the wall, like an art exhibit.

Aside from the opportunity to hear such a diverse group of accomplished musicians in one place, the bonus of getting all the guitars together is to find how many of them are now also related by wood as well as maker. Brandon's cocobolo truss rod cover was made from the wood leftover from Doty's guitar. My own Desio parlor guitar is made from the same Indian rosewood as my husband's semi-baritone.

Between jamming and comparing each other's instruments, Desio talks about the process of building each guitar before introducing its associated performer to play a song. At the most recent gathering at the Bazaar Café, Brandon debuted her new Desio: a piano-top parlor guitar built in part from the leaves of a 19th-century mahogany dining room set that she salvaged from a 2011 house fire that destroyed most of her possessions. She'd bought the table years earlier at the estate sale of a renowned San Francisco madam named Auntie Doris.

Sitting down with her Desio instrument for the first time, she told how she'd learned the madam had once entertained jazz artists and civic leaders at her brothel's table. It was fitting, then, that the pieces of storied mahogany that survived the fire could be given new life as a guitar. ■

CAROLYN McCOY

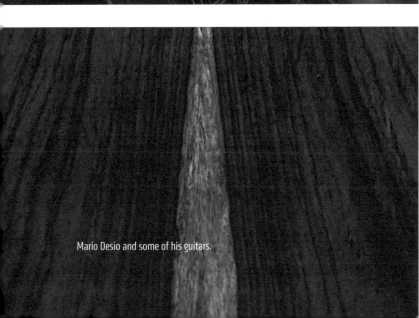

Mario Desio and some of his guitars.

KEEP IT GOIN'

In Levon Helm's barn, a legacy of Rambles

by Anne Margaret Daniel

Memories of eight years of Rambles — those in Woodstock and on the road — loom like a benediction in my head. The Barn has been called a hallowed space by many who performed there, and by those who simply came to hear the music.

RAMBLING AT MIDNIGHT GOES BACK many centuries and encompasses, to put it mildly, a variety of entertainments. The figure of a musician is often involved: the traveling troubadour, instrument slung over his back (almost always, the rambler was a man), rambling the dusty roads from gig to gig, town to town. By the late 17th century, you could ramble in cities as well as towns. To be a midnight rambler had a sexy, dirty connotation: one went out walking after midnight looking for love, or something like it.

John Wilmot, the Earl of Rochester, made crystal clear sometime after 1661 what a "ramble" was all about in his infamous nocturnal saga, "A Ramble in St. James Park," which begins:

Much wine had passed, with grave discourse
Of who fucks who, and who does worse

The Rolling Stones, co-opting the name for their violence-laced 1969 hit "Midnight Rambler," insisted that "it's no rock and roll show." However, this is just what a midnight ramble is and has always been — and the Stones' own hard-riding rock song bears it out, despite the

denial: A midnight ramble is the post-show show, the gig that happens after midnight, when the children have gone to bed and things spice up and get loose.

Just before the First World War, a carnival operator named Fred Swift Wolcott bought a touring variety and music show called, alternately, the Rabbit's Foot Company and the Rabbit Foot Minstrels, from the widow of its founder. Wolcott was a white man, but the company had nearly 70 African-American performers. He added his initials and name to the show, and sent his revue through the South. As it passed through Arkansas, a boy named Levon Helm caught the show, which gave him many fond memories. Years later, Helm transmuted those memories into his song, "The W.S. Walcott Medicine Show."

The cast of characters in The Band's 1970 song includes saints, sinners, losers, and winners — "all kinds of people you might want to know" (note, please, that qualifying *might*). "There's a young faith healer / he's a woman stealer." There's Miss Brer Foxhole, with "bright diamonds in her teeth," who is "pure gold down underneath." And there's the all-American mashup musicians masquerading under the name of "the Klondike Klu Klux Steamboat Band." A late night out at the show is just the thing for you if "your arms are empty" and you've "got nowhere to go."

But the most important words in the song were "medicine show." This is, after all, music with more than a message. It's double-edged, curing what ails you while slipping something into your entertainment, like the miracle-cure medicine shows of the Wild West in the hands of dubious "snake-oil" salesmen touting magical cure-alls. No matter what you thought you bought, you always felt better in the end.

'You Really Should Get Up Here'

At a benefit for guitarist Hubert Sumlin at B.B. King's in New York in 2003, it was a delightful surprise to see Levon Helm settle in behind the drums. Sumlin had recently undergone surgery for lung cancer, and Helm had been contending with the throat cancer he wound up battling for more than a decade. Helm would spend many of those days sitting on stage at his drums or his mandolin, singing when he could; smiling that smile when he could not. During this "Howlin' for Hubert" benefit performance, Helm did not sing, but his drumbeat was as unmistakable and unique as his voice was. He laid down the perfect heartbeat for every song, from the slow, yowling, stripteasy blues to the rockers.

At the end, he stood and cupped his hands. He mouthed, "Yeah, Hubert," at his friend, who turned his back to the cheering crowd and, holding event organizer David Johansen's arm, beamed at Helm. I went home full of love for Hubert and for Howlin' Wolf, but what I put on the record player was "Stage Fright." I wanted to hear Levon sing.

In the summer of 2004, I looked forward to that chance again. Helm had begun to invite friends to make music with him at his house in the woods in Woodstock, New York, on a pond folks now refer to as Lake Levon.

Erik Lawrence played countless Rambles, as the gatherings came to be called, from their ragged beginnings to the very last. "I knew Levon had cancer, and he was doing some pickup blues gigs. I was living in Vermont, and up until

then I'd said yes to what paid, and no to things I wanted to do. Finally I had a little money in the bank, and I called Butch [Dener, longtime road manager for The Band] and said to him, 'Just know anytime Levon's doing a gig, I'll show up and play for free.' And I did.

"Then, one day, Butch called and said, 'You really should get up here!' That was my first Ramble. The band was mostly members of Ollabelle, and Jimmy Vivino. Later on, Levon asked me to 'bring a horn' and I invited Steven Bernstein on trumpet because we played well together off the cuff. When Steven couldn't do it, I'd hire Clark Gayton on trombone because he was such a good musician."

Ollabelle's principal singer was Levon's daughter, Amy Helm. As time went on, she and bassist/composer Byron Isaacs became integral members of the Ramble band. Drummer Tony Leone sat in on drums, as would Amy, occasionally, whenever Levon slid onto the stool at center stage to pick his mandolin.

My first attempt at a Ramble failed. Late on a Saturday afternoon, quite literally as I was leaving my driveway, an older lady in a very large Buick drove into the passenger door of my car, leaving it undrivable. Frantic calls to friends with extra cars got me nothing. I phoned the number given in the confirmation email. A pleasant voice answered — Geanine Kane, who was in charge of merchandise. "Oh, I'll take your name off the list," she said. "Thanks for calling. When would you like to come?" I didn't know what she meant, and had figured I was out close to a hundred bucks (the Ramble price used to be around $90). But she said, "Choose another Ramble. Levon doesn't make people pay for music they don't hear." I picked the following Saturday.

Magic in the Catskills

Woodstock is one of the loveliest little towns — a setting toward which plants, animals, and humans have gravitated

since long before time was recorded. It sits at a little hillcrest on the banks of fast-running creeks Millstream and Tannery Brook, both named for activities that used to take place in the area in the early days of settlement.

Richard Manuel and Rick Danko came to Woodstock in February 1967, as Danko tells it in Helm's *This Wheel's On Fire: Levon Helm and the Story of The Band* (1993). "Richard and I had never been to the Catskills before, and we couldn't believe how beautiful it was," he recounts, "but we were frozen. We went over to Albert Grossman's house and sat in front of a roaring fireplace with his wife, Sally. That was my introduction to Woodstock. As things happened, Sally Grossman would play a key role in our career, and Woodstock would become our home."

After a hiatus from The Band that he spent mostly back home in Arkansas, Helm moved to Woodstock, too. The group started writing songs and singing, sometimes with Bob Dylan and sometimes without, in the basement of a nondescript house in Saugerties that was the color of diluted Pepto-Bismol. They concentrated on vocal harmonies, inspired, Helm recalled, by the Staple Singers and the Impressions, and the way they "would stack those individual voices on top of one another, each voice coming in at a different time until you got this blend that was just *magic*."

That magic vocal blend — with Helm most often singing a discernible lead — became The Band's trademark from 1967 until the original members ceased playing together after their "Last Waltz" in November 1976. Helm kept that magical blend going during the 1980s with Garth Hudson, Rick Danko, and Richard Manuel, who remained Woodstock neighbors for much of the year. They got together at the Joyous Lake, a venue on Tinker Street, and embarked on a world tour in 1983.

All the while, Helm lived in Woodstock with his wife, Sandra. At first, the big barn space was just for him and his friends, a place to make music and record. *The Muddy Waters Woodstock Album*, recorded there in 1975, won a Grammy. After "The Barn" burned to the ground, local craftsmen remade it better, with a high-beamed ceiling and an acoustic cupola at the roof's apex. But Helm did not open the space to regular public concerts until he needed help paying the mortgage on his property. His medical bills for cancer treatment had taken priority.

As Helm told Karen Schoemer of *New York Magazine* in 2007, "I didn't know if I was going to be able to hang onto the place, but I thought, well, I'm going to go out with a bang. I'm going to have as many Rambles as I can, and have as many people as I can get come here and enjoy the music and see the place. And then when they see that I've sold it, they'll know what it was."

Joy and 'The Weight'

Helm was not able to sing the first time I was in the Barn. But, my lord, Alexis P. Suter was. She and her band opened the show with a full-force gale of a set. Suter, in a top hat and a 19th-century-style black gravedigger's ribbon, blew me away with her song "Teacher Man."

"I was there from the fourth or fifth Ramble on," says Suter. She and her band, to which Helm gave the name Alexis P. Suter Band, opened close to a hundred Rambles during the next eight years. "The music went until three or four in the morning. There'd be one person there, and they'd still be playing. It was a never-ending show," she says.

The rest of that night is a blur. I had gotten there early, so I grabbed a chair in the second row, stage left, next to, almost on top of, the drums. I was standing and dancing, so at the interval I offered my seat to an old gentleman in a hat and an electric-blue suit, who was clutching something in his hands. He giggled, and

declined. "I'm performin'," he said. Then: "My name's Sammy. What's yours?"

That was my first encounter with Little Sammy Davis, blues harmonicist extraordinaire.

What I remember best remained a standard at every Ramble I ever attended: Helm's visible, palpable joy about what was happening in his house. He paid attention to every musician, cueing folks to play solos, smiling at them as they played. He looked around the room, from the seats to the standing room to the people leaning over the rails in the rafters, meeting the eyes of his guests. He grinned when he saw you laughing, weeping, or singing along.

And, at the end: "The Weight."

No song, performed live, is ever the same twice, but this is spectacularly, almost eerily, true of "The Weight." The person on the "crazy Chester" verse — usually, though not always, someone who had opened the show — could change the entire song. When Kinky Friedman was at the Ramble, he peered through his half-glasses at the words but couldn't make them out. He laughed, stepped back, and let Larry Campbell take over for him.

When it was Mavis Staples, the Barn was a church. Levon bent over his drums, eyes closed, as if he were praying at an altar.

Memories of eight years of Rambles — those in Woodstock and on the road — loom like a benediction in my head. The Barn has been called a hallowed space by many who performed there, and by those who simply came to hear the music.

We turned Rambles into birthday celebrations: Larry Campbell's and his mother, Maggie's, in the same week, with a sparkler-lit cake. We paid tribute to friends who had passed but were there in spirit. Maggie Campbell's name remains in a front-row chair. There, one night, she rolled her beautiful big eyes as Larry introduced an epic plea from a poor mother with a son in jail, dedicating it to her.

Levon made us all family, which might sound corny, but it's true. On the night he

welcomed his first grandson, he said quietly, "My baby girl done had a baby boy." Cheers of congratulation rained on him and on the tall man in the horn section, Amy Helm's then-husband, Jay Collins. "Papa Jay," Levon shouted out, and that became Collins' name for the evening.

Helm supported his musical guests in atypical and beautiful ways, too. After a sold-out show, Helm called Suter to him. "He went in his pocket and gave me $600, for my mother's church," she remembers. "And [he] said, 'Pray for us. Pray for the Ramble.' And on one of his birthdays, he'd gotten a drum set cake. He said, 'Wrap it up and give it to Alexis for the folks at the church.'" Suter chuckles, remembering how the congregation in another state had enjoyed that.

You bring food to a Ramble — any dish people can enjoy as part of a potluck downstairs before and during the show. The Saturday we learned that Levon's record *Dirt Farmer* had been nominated for a Grammy, I stopped in at Elijah's — a lovely little restaurant, now gone — and the owner tossed a salad. In Sharpie on the Saran Wrap that covered it, he wrote "Levon's Grammy Salad." It was eaten eagerly, as were, on other nights, the homemade venison pate, jambalaya, heirloom tomatoes, roast chicken drumsticks, interestingly flavored and pungent brownies, and Jill Lesh's birthday cake, which had a photo of Phil and Levon on it. When you took a break to sit outside and eat, there might be mosquitoes, or Helm's dogs, Muddy (named for Waters) and Lucy (a stray Levon brought home), keeping you company.

The acoustic Rambles — which happened in 2009 and thereafter, from time to time, on the Friday before a full-on Saturday night — were even more intimate and special, if that was possible. There, Levon played with Amy, Larry, Teresa, Donald Fagen, and old friends who were as good as family: Jimmy Vivino, Mike Merritt, John Sebastian. "And it was in his house," says Suter, "his own

house. You'd go in one of the bathrooms, and there were towels, Listerine, you know. And no one ever took anything."

When Helm began singing regularly again, around 2006, Erik Lawrence remembers, "The press started going crazy about it, and it truly was a medical miracle when his voice came back."

Indeed, famous people started flocking to the Barn. Larry Campbell remembers one night in particular: "Emmylou came and sang," he says. "She was one of the first big stars to come and perform at the Ramble. The career she'd had, and how close she was to Levon, made that one really special."

When Ricky Skaggs came, his tour bus was too big to get down Helm's driveway without incurring scratches from the pine and ash trees. Teresa Williams recalls: "They parked their bus out on the road and walked down that dirt road to the Barn with all their instruments."

Lawrence remembers the night that "Elvis [Costello] and Allen Toussaint just showed up and did a couple of tunes. Then Elvis came onstage when [the Ramble band] first started, and played guitar and sang backgrounds all night. Later, I was talking to Ray LaMontagne and told him about it. He said, 'Yeah, I know, I was there.' He'd bought himself a ticket, and sat by the back wall, and just listened." Indeed, there were as likely to be musical and other celebrities in the crowd as on the stage. Says Campbell, "Billy Bob Thornton came a couple of times. Jane Fonda, Jessica Lange ... it was an easy place to be casual."

No Scene, Just Songs

"[The Rambles] grew from [Levon] digging into his own roots, mostly the blues," says Amy Helm. "He did not

believe in any kind of pretension. It was a scene that had no scene, and the music was on fucking fire."

Jimmy Vivino and Jim Weider used their guitars to fan that fire from the early days. Brian Mitchell, invited up by Erik Lawrence, blazed a blues trail through the sets with his phenomenal piano playing and covers of Dr. John and Bob Dylan, among others. In 2005, Larry Campbell, who had spent the past eight years traveling in Dylan's band, arrived in Woodstock and never left. He became Helm's bandleader, collaborator, and producer, and his modesty about it all surprises no one who knows him.

"I first met Levon at the Lone Star in 1979 or 1980," Campbell says, recalling his early 20s. "I was playing with a bunch of different bands, and I was upstairs in the dressing room, just sitting up there playing the fiddle. Out of the corner of my eye I saw someone standing next

The Ramble Band posing outside
Levon's Barn.

to me, and it was Levon. 'That's some mighty fine fiddling,' he said."

The years passed, but the mutual admiration did not. "Levon and I had a specific rapport," Campbell remembers. "Every time I'd see him, even casually, there'd just be something."

A couple of years later, Helm beckoned Campbell to Woodstock. "I left Dylan's band in January 2005," he says, "and a couple of weeks later, Levon called. He said, 'I heard ya left Bob. Come on up to Woodstock and let's make some music.'"

Campbell and his wife, singer Teresa Williams, bought a home in the area. They settled into the Ramble band and a life together after years on the road — not just apart, but often in different hemispheres. Says Campbell, "After I'd done a couple of Rambles, [Teresa and I] sang together at the Bouche Bar, over on East 5th Street. It was the first time Amy had heard Teresa sing. We'd just begun [Levon's] *Dirt Farmer* record [which Campbell produced], with no real plan to make a record at first, just to record some songs. It was only a matter of weeks before Teresa was a permanent part of the Ramble."

Williams' rich, pure voice and presence onstage not only enriched the Rambles, but reminded you that Helm, though most famous for his all-

male band, welcomed women just as unreservedly, and fostered their careers with all he had. Just ask Alexis P. Suter, Mavis Staples, Carolyn Wonderland, or Grace Potter. Suter says, softly, "He wasn't a man of many words, and when he spoke those words were powerful and insightful. ... I really miss him a lot."

Connections Continue

This past spring, on April 20 (a popular day in the town of Woodstock), some of those women — Amy Helm and Carolyn Wonderland, Shelley King, Marcia Ball, and Cindy Cashdollar — joined bassist Brandon Morrison and drummer Lee Falco at the Barn. Their Texas-Catskill mix sailed under the name of the Woodstock Lonestars, and the show they gave was lovely.

Cowboy boots of fine varieties tapped time onstage, to the beat of Ball's rippling blues and rolling boogie-woogie keyboard and Wonderland's full-tilt Joplinesque performance. However, the day before had marked the fourth anniversary of Levon's passing.

When Amy introduced "a tribute" and began the quiet start of "Atlantic City," the rowdy audience melted into

stillness. King remembered showing up for a Ramble in 2012 that did not happen, after Helm died. She spoke of the huge thunderstorm that hit Woodstock just around 8 p.m. that Saturday night. People sang along with a new song she wrote in the wake of that storm, its final couplet unforgettable:

> *The rhythm of the rain is a*
> *sure-fire bet*
> *Levon's playing his new drum set.*

It was 4/20. There was the sweet-spicy smell of weed in the air outdoors, and Helm, as all who knew him know, would not have objected. Against the rough-planed wood walls, a slim woman with a chic haircut and a brown leather jacket shook her head in time with the music and smiled. It was Sally Grossman, who once upon a time had introduced Rick Danko and Richard Manuel to Woodstock with a good fire on a cold day. Talk about bringing it all back home.

These days, evenings at the barn promise folks like Joan Osborne, Richard Thompson, and Marco Benevento. More dates are announced all the time, regularly, without fanfare — the way Helm liked it.

The Barn physically embodies, and manifests, its life as a performance space and meeting place. It remains a tangible, affirmative response to Helm's deathbed request to "keep it goin'." And, with determination, love, and talent, Amy Helm is determined to heed her father's request.

"I think that it ... will be a place that's open to all kinds of music," she says. "I want musicians to feel good about who they are and what they're doing. ... [The Ramble is] a night where people connect, and forget about things they want to forget.

"That place can hold a lot of music, and it should," she says, adding that, in truth, "It's becoming what it's always been." ∎

"[The Rambles] grew from [Levon] digging into his own roots, mostly the blues. He did not believe in any kind of pretension. It was a scene that had no scene, and the music was on fucking fire." —Amy Helm

John Hiatt joins Helm onstage at the Barn.

Levon Helm and Emmylou Harris.

Levon Helm and Sheryl Crow.

Larry Campbell on guitar, Levon Helm on mandolin.
Opposite: Amy Helm takes the mic.

View of the Barn from Levon's drum kit.

SET ME ON FIRE

L.A.'s Ash Grove was fertile ground for folk music and more

by Kent Gustavson

The club's open policy created an environment where legends of traditional blues, folk, and world music played for, played with, and taught local, urban musicians the tricks of their trade. ... Ry Cooder, Bonnie Raitt, Charlie Musselwhite, Maria Muldaur, Linda Ronstadt, Canned Heat, and Taj Mahal played their first gigs at the Ash Grove.

IN MIDSUMMER 1958, A MODEST, nondescript furniture showroom in West Los Angeles transformed into a broadside-plastered folk music venue that would rapidly change American music history. Over its 15-year life, the Ash Grove exposed an urban audience to a panoply of musical styles, delivered by sometimes legendary, sometimes unknown blues, bluegrass, and folk music greats. The club survived fire-bombing twice, before a third fire destroyed it for good in 1973. At that point, owner Ed Pearl, who had run his establishment more like a charity than a business, decided it was time to finally close the doors. But before that, thousands of other fires ignited between the sonorous walls of the Ash Grove, within the hearts of artists like Mick Jagger and Jim Morrison, Bonnie Raitt and the Byrds, Jerry Garcia and Jackson Browne.

Hootenannies and coffee shops had already hit Los Angeles by the late 1950s, and these were the favored hangouts of poets, intellectuals, and leftists. Unicorn on the Sunset Strip, Cosmo Alley in Hollywood, and other locations sometimes featured folk music, but the Ash Grove started a new standard of eclectic programming that had never existed on the West Coast. Assisted by the Seegers,

friends, former professors at UCLA, and others, Pearl created a music venue that brought disparate races, cultural backgrounds, and musical forms together in a way that had rarely, if ever, existed in such an intimate, accessible setting. The results were explosive — the skilled players who cut their teeth at the Ash Grove became the rock-and-roll pillars of the next generation.

From his office at the Smithsonian Institution in 1987, Ralph Rinzler — widely known for "discovering" Doc Watson and re-establishing Bill Monroe's pre-eminence as the "Father of Bluegrass" — wrote of the importance of the education and exchange that happened within the Ash Grove's walls, between musicians and artists of all kinds: "[The Ash Grove] provided a unique crucible in which cross-cultural exchange could take place as well as a platform for local performers to take the stage alongside seasoned artists of mythic stature," he wrote. "Thus, some of today's internationally known performers benefitted from the most significant formative experiences of their early careers through the open exchange of ideas and sounds which the Ash Grove provided for them both onstage and backstage."

Rinzler added that, due to the reasonable cost of attending concerts at the club, "virtually none were excluded."

The club's open policy created an environment where legends of traditional blues, folk, and world music played for, played with, and taught local, urban musicians the tricks of their trade. Countless young musicians were in that number, and sat wide-eyed in front of their musical heroes. They then had the chance to play for the first time in front of a rapt audience in the small club. Ry Cooder, Bonnie Raitt, Charlie Musselwhite, Maria Muldaur, Linda Ronstadt, Canned Heat, and Taj Mahal played their first gigs at the Ash Grove. Jackson Browne attended as a teenager, David Crosby met Roger McGuinn there, Mick Jagger came to watch Muddy Waters and other blues artists perform, Doc Watson first met and performed with Bill Monroe there, and Bob Dylan wrote in his biography *Chronicles*: "I'd seen posters of folk shows at the Ash Grove and used to dream about playing there."

'Just Wanted to Put on a Show'

"I started the Ash Grove when I was 21, in 1958, because I met somebody [dancer Kate Hughes] and I was sort of wooing her," Ed Pearl says, with nostalgia in his voice.

"We met Carmen Amaya at the Flamingo Club on Sunset Boulevard; she was a great singer, actress, and flamenco dancer — a great artist of the 20th century. She had brought her flamenco troupe to Palm Springs. But when they arrived there, the nightclub folded, so there she was with no money, a gypsy who had to go back to Spain, and the entire troupe was cut loose and stayed in cheap hotels throughout Los Angeles, and hung around this one flamenco club."

Pearl and his girlfriend were smitten by flamenco dance, music, and culture. "The guitar playing and so on was so much better than anything in the folk circles," he recalls, "and I immediately wanted to put on a show for the folk crowd. But the flamenco guitarist I had in mind wouldn't play unless he got 50 dollars. That meant we had to charge money, and that meant that we had to do

a commercial thing. We had just wanted to put on the show for the gang, but this changed everything.

"I looked into finding a really elegant hall, and came across the L.A. Jazz Concert Hall. When I approached him, the proprietor said, 'How much do you think the rent is?'

"Knowing nothing, I said, 'I don't know, 50 dollars?'

"'He chuckled and said, 'Okay, 50 dollars.'

"This was a beautiful 700-seat theater, and we filled it up. So then we put on two more shows, and each one was a full house, with different kinds of things. About that time, everyone was offering me and my girlfriend, Kate, money to book their nightclubs.

"So we went to a nightclub and neither one of us had hardly ever been in a nightclub. We thought surely these were gangsters, and we didn't trust them, so instead we just decided to open our own hall, so that's what we did.

"We converted a big furniture display room and work area into the foyer and concert hall. In the middle were an office and the bathroom. So it was really easy to do the front and the back, and the division was obvious.

"The Ash Grove was relatively small," he adds. "Theoretically, it was supposed to seat something like 200, but we got up to 250 when we had to. It was well planned, so there was rarely a time where people were actually packed in like that. I mean, nowadays in the same space, people would be standing a lot, and there would be far fewer tables. The room capacity would now be between 300 and 400."

The atmosphere at the Ash Grove was different than other venues from the beginning. Roland White recalls first playing at the club with his band, the Country Boys (later renamed the Kentucky Colonels), in 1959. "That's the first time we ever played in that sort of environment," he says. "It was a place where people were listening to music, not

where people were dancing or something like that. It was kind of scary. The audience members were actually looking at us; you could see their faces. It wasn't totally dark. They were actually looking at us and listening. The Ash Grove was just a different thing."

Anthology Brought to Life

The first Ash Grove show took place on July 1, 1958, and featured that flamenco artist, a blues singer, and a folk musician. For a few years, Pearl programmed mainstream artists, but soon he started to feature musicians who represented varied traditions. "The transformation in the Ash Grove really began with Lightnin' Hopkins," he says. "By the time he came, in '60 or '61, the banjo craze had started, the folk craze had started, and people were exploring. And then Tom Paley and the New Lost City Ramblers came and played the music of those cultures. Then, finally, people from the culture themselves came and headlined concerts, such as the Clarence Ashley Group."

One Ash Grove flyer from 1962 proclaims the diversity of the folk club's offerings while trying to sell a discount card to frequent attendees: "[How you will] save money: You break even by coming in 3 times during a year. Thereafter, you save $1 per admission. Figure it out. Will you come in at least three times in a year? That's up to you and the attractiveness of the following artists; all of whom, and maybe others, will be here in 1962." The flyer then breaks the upcoming music into three categories: blues and gospel, traditional bluegrass and country, and international folk music. The lists read as a who's who of talent, from Sonny Terry & Brownie McGhee, Mance Lipscomb, Reverend Gary Davis and Lightnin' Hopkins, to Flatt & Scruggs, Mother Maybelle & the Carter Sisters, Jim & Jesse, and the Country Boys, to international musicians such as Miriam Makeba and Mike Janusz.

Ed Pearl (on top of car) and friends conducting
a voter registration drive near the Ash Grove.

> **"When you're learning an instrument, politics can go to hell. On the other hand, social activism in music is as real a movement as there has been in this country, and I stand behind it being urgent and necessary in culture."**
>
> Ben Harper

Pearl's love of diverse cultures started in college at UCLA, where he studied folklore with Bess Lomax Hawes, among other well-respected and inspiring faculty. Then he was turned on to Harry Smith's curated *Anthology of American Folk Music*, which formed his opinions on the varied and beautiful nature of traditional song. He would model his Ash Grove on this collection, and soon brought a live equivalent of the Anthology to a generation of listeners and learners in Los Angeles.

Pearl's empathy, curiosity, and appreciation of all people pushed him not only to present the artists on the Ash Grove roster, but to educate his audiences about their cultural background and surroundings. With pride, Pearl "would always show the bulletin board with the articles, pictures, and information to the artists and say, 'Well, is there anything here that's wrong or that you don't want me to show?'" He remembers one night when Bill Monroe went up on stage and said, "Now I want you to go outside and I want you to look at what Ed put up there [on the bulletin board]. That's the truth. You're going to see how our people live, and that's good."

Ash Grove Kids

The Ash Grove drew an interested audience of intellectuals, working-class people, kids, and adults. The reasonable door prices and Pearl's generosity kept people coming back for every captivating concert. In particular, Pearl remembers the many talented teenagers and young adults he had a chance to meet and often mentor at the Ash Grove.

"Clarence White and I put in the cedar seats in the back of the Ash Grove," Pearl recalls fondly. "Roland and Clarence White were country boys, and they needed money, so I hired Clarence. He helped me put in all the seats and risers and things like that. I was very close to Clarence. I mean, honestly, very close, like his older brother or something."

Clarence White later went on to revolutionize acoustic and electric guitar. Before his tragic death at the hands of a drunk driver in 1973 (at the age of 29), he had recorded and toured with the Byrds, Muleskinner, and the Kentucky Colonels as well as appearing on countless artists' recordings.

"At 15," Pearl recalls, "Clarence first came to the Ash Grove. He never could stop. As soon as he heard something, he would want to incorporate that into his guitar playing. And so everyone he met and listened to, he would study it, play it, and try to incorporate it. So he was doing all kinds of experimental things from the day I met him. He was a real genius." Much like Clarence White, young Ry Cooder absorbed the eclectic music he heard at the Ash Grove. "[Ry] was dropped off at the front door by his mom, and she even made me Ry's guardian when he was in the Ash Grove," says Pearl. "She was a nurse, and she was very protective, so she wanted to make sure that Ry would be taken care of, you know.

Ry would get there at six o'clock in the evening, or even earlier in the afternoon. His mother would drive him there and he would just wait in the front room until we opened and then he'd buy his ticket and go sit at the counter."

Roland White remembers clearly the counter that stretched around the small stage at the club. "There was the stage, and the stage wasn't really high up off the floor, you know, probably two or three feet. And then there was a counter all the way around it, like an L shape to the left, to the right, and to the wall. And we could just sit there and watch the musicians' hands."

"We put this counter around the stage so it would separate the stage from the audience," Pearl remembers. "And of course, it was also a counter, so people could sit right there next to the musicians. The lip of the counter was higher than the stage. That place quickly became the property of all of the people who were learning how to play."

Sitting around that stage over the years was a long list of future stars. Besides Clarence White, Roland White, and Ry Cooder, some of the "youngsters" who sat only inches from their favorite performers included Bonnie Raitt, David Lindley, Richard Greene, and Jerry Garcia.

Legendary mandolinist David Grisman recalls the group of young up-and-coming musicians at the time. "Like David Lindley and Ry Cooder, we were all around the same age," Grisman says. "We were all, you know, World War II babies."

Taj Mahal was one of the Ash Grove kids, too, and remembers his old friend Clarence White making quite the impression. "Everybody else was playing their D-28 or D-45," he says. "Clarence was playing a D-18, and playing it damn well. I'm telling you, it was boogying. Clarence could play it traditional, but he also wanted to play rock, and he wanted to rock it. That's what later turned into the Flying Burrito Brothers and all of that. I mean, look what he did. He was just amazing."

Roland White remembers when Garcia, only a few years older, came to visit. "I met Jerry Garcia before he had the Grateful Dead," White says. "He and Sandy Rothman came down to the Los Angeles area and saw us play. They mostly spent time with Clarence, but while we were playing at the Ash Grove, he was really impressed with the band; especially Clarence's guitar playing. He introduced us one night at the Ash Grove and said, 'America's best young bluegrass band, the Kentucky Colonels.'"

Guitarist Tony Rice remembers sitting at the Ash Grove's counter, seeing both Clarence White (then 19) and Doc Watson (then 40), his two biggest influences. "I saw Doc at the Ash Grove in '63," he says. "Of course I was only 12 years old, but still very much interested in music and playing and mostly hanging out with the White brothers, you know, Clarence and Roland. My perception of Doc Watson at the time when I first heard him play was that for me to be able to play a guitar like that was unattainable. Of course, I also felt the same way about eventually playing like Clarence White. It took me well into my teens to figure out that I couldn't play like either one of them anyway, which turned out to be good. As a result, I sort of followed my own path."

With emotion laced into his deep, now-broken voice, Rice adds, "If I had to describe how they were an influence on me, I would say that they raised the bar real, real, real damn high."

Rice wasn't the only one who saw that bar being set. Pearl was amazed by the influence his small folk club was having on talented young musicians. "We had all these young people," he says. "Teenagers were immediately enraptured by all this stuff. And it just ... it changed. I mean, it changed right there."

West Coast Circuit

In the early '60s, countless folk clubs emerged up and down the West Coast, and a stint at the Ash Grove could support an entire West Coast tour for a traveling musician or folk group. One stop on such a tour was the Golden Ring, a folk music cafe in Claremont, California, about 30 miles east of Los Angeles.

Starting in 1961, Grammy-winning singer-songwriter Ben Harper's grandparents — Dorothy and Charles Chase — hosted the folk and blues greats of the day in their music series, including Watson, Reverend Gary Davis, John Fahey, Sonny Terry and Brownie McGhee, the New Lost City Ramblers, and many more. The Chases had been operating their Folk Music Center in Claremont as a means of featuring musical instruments, classes, and more. But for five years during the folk boom, they featured live performances as well.

"It was one of the main Southern California folk music stops on the circuit," Harper says. "[They'd] host musicians ... then they would stay at my grandparents' house. That was the folk tradition back then, you'd stay at the house of the people hosting you."

Ben's mother, Ellen Chase Verdries, remembers many varied houseguests. "We constantly had people there," she says. "It was a very interesting way to grow up. We even had people camped out in the backyard in tents. I just kind of took it all in as a child, you know, it just sort of seemed like the way it was. I was aware that it was an extremely different

kind of lifestyle than what my friends had, but it just felt pretty normal."

Verdries recalls the importance of cultural diversity at the club. In particular, she remembers a conversation her parents had about Doc Watson and Clarence Ashley, who were staying in their home at the time. "One of the things I can remember was my parents talking when they didn't know that their children were eavesdropping on them. I recall a conversation about how amazing it was that Clarence and Doc could sit in a room; there could be people of any race there, and there didn't seem to be any blatant racism at all, you know. And yet here they were from the South."

The Chase family had only recently arrived in California. Verdries explains, "My father was a school teacher, and someone who was raised on a farm and grew up knowing how to do everything, like farm boys do, so he was a great fix-it guy. And my mother was an artist and musician. We left New England because my father had been fingered by the House Un-American Activities Committee in the McCarthy period, and he was unable to find work because he wouldn't 'talk' about other artists. He was blacklisted. They would publish your address in the paper, so we had people throwing rocks at the house. And when he couldn't find work, he decided to just pick up roots and family and all and move west. I was seven when that happened, but I remember because it was very traumatic for the family. So we came out here, and landed in Claremont.

"My father got his teaching credentials in Claremont and started teaching," she adds. "But within literally months of getting here, a few things started happening. First, my parents were amassing musical instruments every which way. They used to go out and find them at swap meets and junk stores, and my mother, of course, had her own collection of banjos and guitars. And second, they realized there was nowhere for us to sit down anymore in the house, because

Top left: Clarence White and Richard Greene. Top right: The Country Boys. Center left: Brownie McGhee and Sonny Terry. Center right: Doc Watson sitting in with Clarence Ashley. Bottom: The counter surrounding the stage at the Ash Grove, where Taj Mahal, Bonnie Raitt, and others watched and learned.

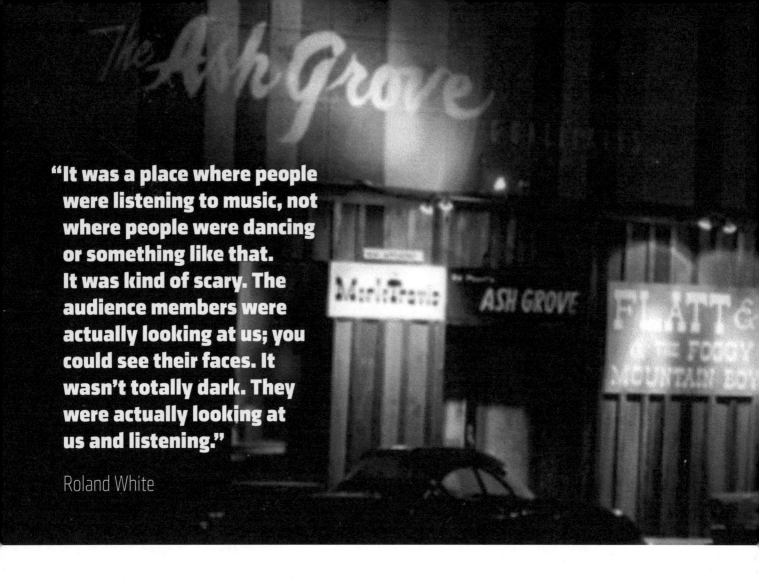

"It was a place where people were listening to music, not where people were dancing or something like that. It was kind of scary. The audience members were actually looking at us; you could see their faces. It wasn't totally dark. They were actually looking at us and listening."

Roland White

there were so many instruments. So they said, 'Let's start a store.' And they started a teeny tiny store that grew very rapidly."

Once they added the folk music cafe in 1961, they hosted many guests at their home, from John Fahey to the giants of the blues. "I remember Brownie McGhee and Sonny Terry, because they were also just terrific houseguests and very gracious and delightful. We also had Reverend Gary Davis at the house. That was quite an experience because he was a pretty far-gone alcoholic, and that was a little hard to deal with. But, you know, we were sort of on the circuit."

Tradition Is a Way of Life

There was an indelible connection between the stops on the West Coast folk music circuit, whether festivals or the

dozens of folk clubs that sprouted up, much like the Golden Ring, supported by musicians who were driven by passion for the music and culture. And the circuit always started at the Ash Grove.

When she was a teenager, Verdries would go to the Ash Grove by any means possible: "I just remember feeling like it was, you know, sort of the mecca for folk music. I mean, everybody played there that I ever wanted to hear. And you know, it was just very exciting; lots of fun, especially for a young person. I would hitch a ride with anybody I could, any way I could. And my parents often took me, when they were there."

Verdries describes her younger self as "a little bit of a freak, actually. In the early '60s, the girls had bubble hair, and I had long black hair down to my waist." But she found a community among the folk musicians all around her: "I would leave

school every day in junior high and high school and walk down to the store and help my grandfather in the store, so I had a bunch of friends from there. I would just hang around and meet with musicians all day."

Dorothy and Charles Chase connected their daughter Ellen to the pipeline of musical tradition, and Ellen connected her son, Ben, to that same pipeline. Ellen, a single mother who plays several instruments, would take Ben to her gigs with her, and he spent afternoons at his grandparents' store, surrounded by music.

Ben Harper first saw a Weissenborn lap steel guitar being played in the hands of David Lindley, and had his first gig with Taj Mahal. "Without [Taj's] attention to the tradition, I might not be here today," says Harper. "Taj keeps the music alive by playing it, because it's as timeless as the mountains — as tall as the mountains and as wide as rivers."

Speaking to his own performance and adaptation of traditional music with such collaborators as the Blind Boys of Alabama, Ben Harper says, "[The music] connects you, it links you, it does a lot of things. It deems you worthy of carrying the flame of the tradition. You become a part of passing that tradition down. That honor is not to be approached lightheartedly.

"Whether it's Pete Seeger, Doc Watson, or the Blind Boys of Alabama," he adds, "they are what made the folk tradition. They're what enabled the folk tradition and blues and gospel tradition to thrive into the next hundred years. If it weren't for them, [the tradition] wouldn't have [survived]. And so to be connected to it, to be considered part of its family, in my generation, is a responsibility. It's a musical responsibility. The good part is that it's [also] a natural responsibility. It's where I'm supposed to be. It feels like family. It just feels great to be a part of that tradition."

Echoing the legacy of his mother and his grandparents, Harper adds, "Tradition is not only a responsibility — it's a way of life."

Burn One Down

The folk movement was not just about music, culture, and tradition, though. It was also about politics. Ed Pearl's Ash Grove eventually suffered the consequences of its political involvement, but he felt that this club should be a place that represented all people — and stood for all people.

The club hosted cultural events with films, photographs, art, and music. It hosted political benefits. It was a meeting place for the Black Panthers, Students for a Democratic Society, and the Young Socialist Alliance, as well as for Pearl's own Peace & Freedom Party. During the Vietnam War, it was a rallying point for buses that were headed to Berkeley and San Francisco for demonstrations there, and during the battle for civil rights it was a rallying point for buses full of Freedom Riders headed to the Deep South. The club supported women's rights and voting rights for 18-year-olds. In the late '60s, it screened films in support of Fidel Castro and his revolution in Cuba. In fact, Pearl believes anti-Castro groups were responsible for the three fires that eventually put the folk music club out of business in 1973.

The activism of the Ash Grove and other folk clubs of that time encouraged its regulars to become politically engaged, to go out and change the world. Ben Harper has picked up that legacy as well. During a recent concert at a California university, Harper said from the stage, "I'm not gonna take all the credit, but I'd like to think I played a small role in California's liberal stance." Indeed, his international hit, "Burn One Down," proclaims, "My choice is what I choose to do / And if I'm causing no harm it shouldn't bother you."

Offstage, Harper says of music and politics, "My take is: instrument first [and] song first. And that's the most important. I mean, when you're learning an instrument, politics can go to hell, to be honest with you. When you're wood-shedding and putting the notes to the scales, and the dexterity that it takes, you know, I mean everything else pretty much stops.

"On the other hand, social activism in music is as real a movement as there has been in this country, and I stand behind it being urgent and necessary in culture. … For me, it's necessary and it's crucial."

Another World

A few miles away from the Golden Ring, down the street from the Ash Grove, rock music found a solid foothold. On the Sunset Strip, the Lovin' Spoonful, Buffalo Springfield, and the Byrds took root, and in the Troubadour club, folk turned to rock as David Crosby, Jackson Browne, Linda Ronstadt, and others made it their home. The Mamas and the Papas came soon after, and the Rolling Stones, Bob Dylan, and Sonny and Cher were filling the Hollywood Bowl. Through it all, the Ash Grove remained a mecca for the cultural traditions that fueled the new strains of popular music that were coming to define the California sound.

The late Mike Seeger once told me how important traditional music was in the development of urban performance. "This music was new to people in the city; it was a revelation to them," he said. And Seeger was a frequent artist at the Ash Grove with his band, the New Lost City Ramblers. He often helped Pearl book new acts, particularly in the early years of the Ash Grove.

Jerry Garcia came to the Ash Grove to hear Scotty Stoneman play the fiddle. Clarence Ashley took the licks he learned from Doc Watson there, electrified them, made them his own, and brought them down the street, changing the sound of the Byrds and countless other bands — and modern music in the process.

"The artists had to walk through the place and say 'hello,'" Pearl recalls. "The only bit of film on the Ash Grove that still exists is a Muddy Waters concert in 1972, and you see Muddy walking through the audience. And one person after another came up to shake his hand, so it took him like five minutes to get onstage because of everyone [greeting him] like that. And then the audience would just hang around with the staff and people that they met there. It wasn't like a regular nightclub."

Indeed, the Ash Grove was the place where legends sat next to kids, stars sat next to hippies, blue collar workers sat next to professors, and where the world shifted on its axis a little bit with every tune. ∎

THE ORIGINAL FOLK PUNK

How Martin Carthy's legacy inspired a new generation of UK folk

by Cara Gibney

BELFAST, IRELAND, IN 1978 WAS a markedly different place than Belfast today. Violence kept people off the street, scared. But there were enlightened souls who carried a torch and kept doors open, despite the times. They offered an alternative.

The late Geoff Harden — who ran the Sunflower Folk Club on Corporation Street — was one of them. It was not easy for him to find artists who would set foot in Belfast, but he managed it, booking some of the most respected acts on the circuit as well as up-and-comers, all of whom he lovingly recorded on reel-to-reel tape. There was, for example, Paul Brady, Ralph McTell, a 16-year-old Sharon Shannon — who made quite an impression — and Londoner Martin Carthy.

Carthy played Sunflower Folk Club in late October 1978, and his performance

> ## "There's a wonderful arrogance to being young. We really thought that we'd discovered something. In fact we had."
>
> Martin Carthy

that night was released in 2011 as the live solo album *The January Man.* In the background of the record, you can hear chatting and glasses clinking. Although the folk icon had traveled from London to a conflicted Belfast that night, in many ways he was at home.

Carthy is regarded by many as the godfather of English folk music, and is potentially its finest composer, interpreter, performer, protector, and innovator. A key figure in English folk since the 1960s folk revival, and a leading light during it, the guitarist and singer worked the folk clubs with a sense of shared ownership and a lack of artifice that he carries to this day.

Award-winning folk musician and composer Chris Wood has been a passionate devotee of traditional music and dance since 1990, and a close

collaborator with Carthy. "Back in the day, [Martin's] impact was seismic," he says of the man with whom he served a virtual "apprenticeship."

"There were thousands of folk clubs in Britain at that time and most of them had a Carthy impersonator," he adds. "I played the fiddle *because* I didn't want to be seen as a Carthy clone. Only years later did I feel I had earned the guitar — my first love."

A strong solo artist, Carthy is also renowned for collaborations such as his part in pioneering folk-rock band Steeleye Span and a long-time partnership with fiddler Dave Swarbrick, who also played with Fairport Convention. He is the father figure in a family of music royalty. Carthy's wife, Norma Waterson, is a doyenne of British folk, having started her career with the renowned

traditional folk group the Watersons (in which Carthy also played) and working over the decades both solo and in collaborations. She was awarded an MBE (Member of the Order of the British Empire) for her services to folk music in 2003, five years after Carthy received the same honor. Their daughter, the singer-songwriter and multi-instrumentalist Eliza Carthy, was awarded an MBE in 2014.

Fabulously Arrogant

When Carthy was a child, his father, Albert, worked for the Trades Union Congress for years, but he also "harbored a secret love for traditional music," Carthy says. "My dad played the fiddle but I never realized what he played. Of course, being East End working-class [and] Anglo-Irish, he played the Irish fiddle, but he gave up because my mum didn't like it."

Carthy's mother, Toby, was a committed Christian socialist. "I think she was a teenager when [her activism] started in the 1930s," he says, adding that as her children were born, her activism waned. "She completed an apprenticeship as a journalist. She really wanted to write — and she *could* write — but she gave that up to have children and bring them up. So she was disappointed, put it that way. ... Of course she loved me and my sister, but it stopped her dream. These days people can do both, [but back] then it was tough."

When Carthy left school at the age of 17, he worked in theater before taking up a residency in the Troubadour folk club in London. By that stage, of course, he believed he had acquired the skills necessary for the role of a residential folksinger. "There's a wonderful arrogance to being young," he says with a chuckle. "We really thought that we'd discovered something. In fact we had, and we were standing up on stage learning an instrument, learning how to sing on the hoof. ... There were some people who were much better than we were, technically, and they were making fun of us all the time. We just shrugged and thought, 'You don't know. You don't get it.' And no, they didn't [get it]. But we knew that we did." He laughs. "[We were] fabulously arrogant, but it got us excited."

Hearing Carthy talk about the arrogance and excitement of making folk music as a young man, it's easy to detect a vague whiff of punk to it all. Indeed, both he and Norma Waterson's early musical manifestations were in the punk-like skiffle movement. "[Skiffle] was wonderful because it put music into the hands of hundreds of thousands — if not millions — of ordinary people," an animated Carthy explains. "The next time that happened with the same energy, and I recognized that energy ... [was with] the Sex Pistols. That was exactly the same thing. [They were] the people taking music back from the machine and doing it themselves. The Pistols were fabulous."

The relationship between folk music and punk is something Kate Stables — the multi-instrumentalist frontwoman of folk-rock collective This Is The Kit —

sees as well. "The artists that do appeal to me," she says, "often have in common the simple punk approach of just getting up and singing their hearts out, either from personal stories or more political ones. It's something I see in the music of people like Martin Carthy and Peggy Seeger and Dick Gaughan ... I feel like [Martin is] one of the original folk punks."

It's the balance of personal and political that drew Carthy to folk music in the first place. "Those big narrative ballads," he says, "they don't half tell you about people. [They're] political in the most personal sense. And people — because [the ballad is] there, and it's been there for a long time — think that by nature it's old hat."

Chris Wood puts it another way: "The big ballads reveal the selfish [people] to be nothing more than they are. They give the immoral character time to plot and to show their hand. They give time for the ordinary person to discover the hero inside themselves and to prevail."

Within those traditional verses, the full gamut of human emotion and behavior is writ large: love, death, kindness, hate, treachery, cruelty, lust. "I like [Martin's] draw toward the darker stories and songs that show a seedier side of society sometimes," Stables says. "[They're] truly human stories. [There's] darkness but a sense of humor also."

Updating Tradition

Indeed, humor and humanity — and, ultimately, optimism — are elements that keep English folk music alive, and pertinent. "One thing that's noticeable about English folk songs," Carthy explains, "is that you can say absolutely anything you like about the relationship between a man and a woman. You can tell all sorts of horrific stories as long as, in the end, they get married and live happily ever after."

The album Carthy recorded that night in Belfast, *The January Man*, consists of 13 tracks of mostly traditional fare. One of them is his update of the Child ballad "Prince Heathen." In it, the prince wants his way with a fair maiden. When she says no, he imprisons her, rapes her, starves and humiliates her, and kills her family. After she gives birth to his child, he decides he loves her.

*"Oh I killed your father in his bed
and your mother by his side
And your seven brothers one by one,
I drowned them in the tide
O lady will you weep for me, lady
tell me true"
"Oh never yet, you heathen dog,
I never shall for you"*

It is an important song to Carthy, and it drives home the importance of a man understanding the word "no." "'Prince Heathen' is the one that really woke me up to that idea," he says. "It's a terrifying song. ... This lady has been saying no all the way through it and it just struck me that it can't end [that way]. She has to go on saying no, because this man is dreadful."

UK singer-songwriter Emily Portman agrees that a lot of the old songs carry with them antiquated ideas about not only gender roles, but other cultural taboos as well. "There are a few folk songs that get left by the wayside as societies change and beliefs shift," she says. "There are songs that are refreshingly subversive and songs we'd rather forget about, that endorse wife-beating or vilify Jews. So in those cases it sometimes feels appropriate to update or rewrite a song. It's interesting how the same song can take on different meanings, depending on who's singing it."

Songs written epochs ago can summon emotions and address stark realities that we're still facing today. That's one truth contemporary English folksingers are learning from the legacy Carthy has handed to them. "[Carthy] has kept faith with the wisdom and genius of those anonymous songwriters who have gone before," says Chris Wood. "Those songs mean something to the young, but they take on a whole other meaning as you grow old. Martin has stayed with them, trusted them. He's never cut a corner, never sought or adhered to a 'winning formula.' In a world of pretenders, Martin is the real thing."

Indeed, Martin Carthy believed music had a job in Belfast in '78, just as it has a job now: to act as a vehicle for getting a message across, for connecting people. "Music has to challenge you," he says. "[It has to] make you snigger, make you giggle, make you cross. Music has to be free." ∎

HARD TIMES IN OLD ENGLAND

**Modern artists plumb the depths
of England's folk tradition**

by Stephen M. Deusner

Josienne Clarke and Ben Walker.

> **"Two hundred or 300 years ago, people were moaning about the same things: taxes, poverty, money, immigration, stuff like that. Life is exactly the same now as it was then. It's history repeating itself. So it's really important for us to make that link to the past."**
>
> Nicola Kearey (Stick in the Wheel)

NICOLA KEAREY'S VOICE IS A remarkable thing: powerful and barbed, pitched somewhere between Shirley Collins and Johnny Rotten. She sings with her blunt city accent intact: not the posh lilt of the upper classes, but a rougher cadence that turns "feather bed" into "fehver bed" and "country" into "cuncher-ee." As frontwoman of the London-based band Stick in the Wheel, Kearey doesn't just sing songs. Standing with her eyes closed and her arms crossed, she channels the ghosts of long-dead, long-forgotten Londoners — the men and women whose lives are rarely recounted in history books or museum exhibitions.

"This is a song about the London Riots," she tells an audience at the Village Folk — a monthly concert series at the Lawns Hotel in Chellaston, just outside of Derby — before Stick in the Wheel launch into their song "Me N Becky." Kearey squeezes out a jittery two-step on her red concertina, then the rest of the band join in: Si Foote banging a steady rhythm on what looks like a drum case, Ellie Wilson adding slivers of fiddle, and Ian Carter repeating a spidery riff on his Dobro. Kearey and co-vocalist Fran Foote create slightly discordant, discomfiting harmonies as they recount the story of a woman and her friend joining the street frenzy that came with the 2011 riots in Tottenham, after white police officers killed a black man.

Unexpectedly, the song starts with a bit of humor and the crowd chuckles at the lines, "Strangest shopping I'd ever seen / No one got a receipt!" There are louder laughs when Kearey describes nicking a TV then stowing it in a Dumpster when it gets too heavy to carry. But everyone grows quiet as the song progresses and turns dead serious. The nature of the crimes weighs heavily on the narrator, and her conscience keeps her awake all night ("Man I felt so sorry / some people lost their homes"). The song wends its way through the narrative until the narrator lands in jail, wondering if she'll ever see her young daughter again. "Becky says she's doing fine," Kearey laments, as the song winds down, and she delivers the final line to a silent room: "But she ain't the one sat here doing time."

A new composition that nevertheless sounds like it could have been sung for a century, "Me N Becky" is a bold and harrowing dissection of class and crime in England, from its tragicomic storyline to Kearey's anguished performance. It's the lynchpin of a spirited gig at the Village Folk, a program established in November 2014 by a local man named Stephen Coles and run by his family.

The idea of the series is an update on the 1950s and '60s music clubs and folk nights that transformed neighborhood gathering spots into music venues, took over supper clubs, or fashioned someone's living room or basement into a makeshift stage. While there are no opening acts or floor spots — which typically allow nonprofessionals to sing a song, recite a poem, or tell a few jokes — there are two 45-minute sets with a long intermission between, during which most of the audience heads to the hotel bar.

It's a long way from the touring circuit most bands travel. The crowd might be small — Stick in the Wheel typically draws ten times as many listeners elsewhere — but the space is intimate, the mood casual and convivial. As the evening proceeds, the crowd grows increasingly boisterous, loosened up, perhaps, by the house ale. They clap and sing, they joke with the band between songs. When the band's version of the 18th-century jobless lament "Hard Times" rolls around, the small crowd provides rough, robust harmonies on the chorus, raising pints in the air:

> *Hard times in old England!*
> *Very hard times!*

It's an adventurous set that mixes new songs like the land-rights anthem "Common Ground" with reworkings of folk standards and centuries-old tunes like "Four Loom Weaver" (which dates back to the Napoleonic Wars). There's a song based on 18th-century street cries, another about Victorian prostitutes who pick their clients' pockets. London emerges through all these songs as a grim but lively place.

By the end of the night, the crowd isn't satisfied with the two sets and encore of "Barbara Allen." At the request of Village Folk's founder, Stick in the Wheel runs through "Me N Becky" one more time, with the crowd joining in, raucously. If we typically think of folk music as looking to the past, every singer

at the Village Folk — amateur and professional alike — keeps it anchored in the present.

Sung by Many Mouths

This idea — that the past in England is as present as ever — seems to be the ethos of a new generation of English folk artists, who, like Stick in the Wheel, are plumbing a millennium of national history and folklore to figure out the 21st century. Arguably, they draw upon more history than any previous generation: not just the full range of English folk culture, but a series of popular revivals as well. In other words, these artists build upon the myriad ways folk music has been defined, approached, written, rewritten, and performed, even as they add their own innovations. To be a folk musician in England, especially at this moment, means becoming a historian, assembling new songs from old scraps.

A few of these artists have flirted with mainstream success: London-based singer and song collector Sam Lee earned a Mercury Prize nomination for his 2012 album *Ground of Its Own*. (He lost to Alt-J.) Jim Moray recorded an album of folk songs in modern arrangements as a doctoral dissertation, only to watch it become a surprise best-seller and propel him from academic to pop star.

Some are lifers, like the folk orchestra Bellowhead; others hail from dynasties, like Eliza Carthy, the daughter of Norma Waterson and Martin Carthy. Most struggle in the underground, playing folk clubs and small venues around the British Isles and Ireland, occasionally touring the continent or, if they're especially ambitious, the States. Most play to older folks who might have been around to catch an early Fairport Convention show or who might remember watching John Martyn on the Kingston Folk Barge. Much like their counterparts in the US, England's younger listeners are always discovering the music and what it means.

Any efforts to pin the scene to one city or one club, to make it coalesce around a single location or artist, would be futile. There is no centralized folk scene in England, but a loosely bound collection of smaller scenes struggling to succeed, sometimes against one another and often against a public misperception of what folk music actually is. No folk artist working today enjoys the popularity of Mumford & Sons or Ed Sheeran, both of whom are regularly described by media and fans as folk but actually have little to do with the form or its traditions. Mumford is a rock band in old-time clothing, while Sheeran is a singer-songwriter whose lyrics veer toward pop confessional — like a boy-band version of James Taylor. Both of these acts might play acoustic instruments, but neither plays true folk music. There is no history behind their songs, which are new not only in the sense that they were written recently but also in the sense that they adhere to modern song forms and sentiments.

True English folk music, as much as any art form can be called "true," is difficult to define, but it is based on older forms, takes older shapes, borrows older melodies, and is freighted with a history that extends far beyond the person performing it. Folk music literally implies folks: music about people, made by people. Its concerns have been historically communist, certainly populist, and arguably humanist, whether tackling issues that directly affect ordinary people (land rights, poverty) or participating in a shared identity. Folk music typically has not one author, but multitudes. Each song is shaped by many hands, sung by many mouths.

This history makes the English folk scene all the more interesting. In the mid-2010s, folk is a music in the throes of vigorous reappraisal and reinvention, which allows artists to innovate and experiment away from the glare of the public eye, with few concessions to popular demands or

Stick in the Wheel (L to R): Ellie Wilson, Fran
Foote, Nicola Kearey, Si Foote, Ian Carter.

to celebrity expectations. In some ways, it's ironic that such a populist music could be as unpopular as it is today, but the form thrives on the fringes, where it can accentuate regional differences and personal eccentricities. Thus, English folk music is as exciting now as it has ever been.

History Repeating

"If someone had said to me 30 years ago that I would be doing folk music, I would have been like, 'What the hell?'" Kearey says, two weeks after the Village Folk show. She and Carter — they are Stick in the Wheel's two founding members — are sitting in the cafeteria at the Wellcome Collection in London, which seems worlds away from the Lawns Hotel. This modern museum of medical artifacts was named for the philanthropist/entrepreneur Sir Henry Solomon Wellcome, a pioneer in the pharmaceutical business. The cafeteria sprawls across the length of the ground floor, its windows looking out on the throngs of tourists hurrying down Euston Road. The clatter of silverware on porcelain and the chatter of museumgoers discussing the current exhibition on human consciousness create a wall of white noise around us.

"It's not a cool thing to do," she continues. "It's something to be embarrassed about, because English people do not value their own culture. Specifically working-class traditions. We're encouraged not to. We've very much encouraged instead to aspire to middle class and basically shit on the working classes."

For Stick in the Wheel, folk music is not merely a calling. Rather, it is a vocation, a skilled trade. In the age of digital media and stunted album sales, the group's sound is defiant in its steadfast belief in folk music as a bullhorn for the common people. "I'm not explicitly political in that way," Kearey claims at

one point, but the band's music certainly has a political bite: Although they might be hundreds of years old, songs like "Four Loom Weaver" have a great deal to say about how we calculate the worth of human labor today.

> *I'm a four loom weaver as many*
> *a man knows*
> *Naught to eat and I've worn out*
> *my clothes.*

Operating four looms simultaneously took incredible skill and coordination, but it barely paid enough to put clothes on a bent back. Toil is the band's true subject, which has earned them a reputation as the scene's prickliest punks. "There might be friction with people who don't like us for whatever reason, because we don't do folk music the way they think it should be done, or they think our music is too raw, too hard on the ears," says Kearey. "That's fine. I don't care."

And yet they are only recent practitioners of the form. Friends since sixth form college (more or less equivalent to American high school), Kearey and Carter have been playing together for more than a decade, yet their earliest collaborations bear little resemblance to the music they make today. After a brief stint in the indie rock band Barefoot Contessa, Carter launched a dubstep project called Various Production, through which he released a series of dance-oriented albums and singles in the mid- and late 2000s.

"That's when we decided to do the folk stuff really raw and stripped back, because we had done all the weird electronic stuff," says Carter. "Most people go the other way 'round [and] add all these little things to a folk song. But we started off doing all this mad stuff and then decided to make those rhythms and sounds with acoustic instruments rather than syncing up a loop." Nonetheless, Carter approaches the guitar like he's working a sequencer, playing short, repeating themes that form the essential

rhythmic foundations for Stick in the Wheel songs. The effect can be mesmerizing, allowing the band to hit weird grooves and lending the acoustic instruments a grittiness that sounds distinctively urban.

In 2015, the group self-released its full-length debut, *From Here*, and it's one of the most bracing, at times abrasive folk albums of the new century: a collection of hardscrabble tunes that portray London life then and now as a constant struggle. "Our intent," says Kearey, "is to show that 200 or 300 years ago, people were moaning about the same things: taxes, poverty, money, immigration, stuff like that. Life is exactly the same now as it was then. It's history repeating itself. So it's really important for us to make that link to the past."

"When you're doing commercial music, you're doing it for yourself. It's for your own personal gain," adds Carter. "But when you do music that's about the culture, it's for the personal gain of everybody."

Collecting at the Cecil Sharp House

"You've probably heard talk of folk revivals," says Nick Wall. He and Laura Smyth are sitting at a table in the Vaughan Williams Memorial Library, a small room in London's Cecil Sharp House. Around them are towering black bookshelves stuffed with thousands of volumes: folk song collections, histories, critical analyses, biographies, autobiographies. Three desks support leaning columns of papers and CDs and a few turntables of various vintages. Every horizontal surface holds a book of some sort; every vertical surface is covered by black-and-white photographs of Frankie Armstrong looking commanding onstage or A.L. "Bert" Lloyd and Ewan MacColl engaged in a duet, their arms draped over one another's shoulder.

"The revival of the 1950s and 1960s is actually the second one," explains Wall, assistant librarian. "The first one in England is called the Golden Age of Song Collecting, going from about 1880 through the First World War, around 1914. Cecil Sharp was one of the most prolific collectors in that revival."

At this modest brick building in the Camden neighborhood of London, a small battery of librarians — including Wall and Smyth, who serves as library and archives director and is a supremely talented folksinger herself — continue the work Sharp started more than a century ago.

Born in Surrey, educated at Cambridge, and at one time living in Australia, Sharp worked as a music teacher at a school north of London at the turn of the 20th century. His destiny as a song collector, however, was set when he heard the local vicarage gardener — a man improbably named John England — singing a song called "The Seeds of Love." By bicycle and train, Sharp set off around the British Isles to find similar songs sung by common English folk, working men and women in rural villages and coastal communities. His travels took him around Europe and even across the Atlantic to Appalachia, where he collected American songs usually just one generation removed from England. By his death in 1924, he had transcribed more than 5,000 folk tunes — long before recording sound waves on wax discs or acetate was a practical option.

Roughly a century later, Sharp remains an imposing figure in the contemporary English folk scene, not because he was the first song collector, nor even because he was by far the most prolific. Instead, his truest legacy may be his insistence that folk culture is essential to the English national identity — a notion that inspired him to campaign for its inclusion in school curricula, to publish such books as *English Folk Song: Some Conclusions* (1907), and to establish in 1911 what is now known as the English Folk Dance and Song Society (EFDSS).

In that regard, Sharp has influenced many generations of folk artists and song collectors. Ralph Vaughan Williams used many of these songs as the foundation for his classical compositions, as did many of his contemporaries and followers throughout the first half of the 20th century. Says Smyth: "They were finding these beautiful songs still being sung by the rural working class, and they were using them for their own inspiration and for their own compositions. They thought that by teaching children these songs, it would make our nation better and would make everyone lovely and happy."

As Smyth speaks, the walls of the library reverberate with stomps and shouting. Discordant voices rise and fall in a muffled din. She explains that a drama troupe is rehearsing in the next room; elsewhere in the building a choir is warming up. The EFDSS rents these facilities to musicians, actors, dancers, and artists in every medium. This is not a quiet library, but the din seems appropriate to the subject of study here: The Cecil Sharp House remains a hub for the arts community, even if that community is dispersed across London and throughout England.

Making It Sexy

In Birmingham's New Street train station, a cavernous ultramodern structure that resembles a disco seedpod on the outside and a '60s futuristic spaceship on the inside, Sam Lee tells me about a conference on the Gypsy Traveler culture that he has just left. "I've spent a day talking about the inherent racism of this country and its attitudes toward this culture," he says, then admits, "It was really good that I was there."

Lee is a busy man. He'll rush away shortly to catch a train back to London. He has a band rehearsal this evening in preparation for an upcoming gig.

In some ways, he is the heir of Cecil Sharp, although he would certainly reject such a mantle. Among the foremost song

collectors of his day, Lee is a tireless listener and amanuensis whose subject is the great Romany Traveler communities that have endured on the margins of British society for centuries. They're better known by the common pejorative "gypsies," and it is toward them that the aforementioned "inherent racism" is projected. Most live in the English equivalents of reservations, nomadic people crammed into government housing or living under motorways or along roadsides.

"I'm going into poverty-stricken areas, into homes and trailers and caravans," Lee explains. "Invariably these people are wonderful and welcoming, but what I'm facing is a great silencing of a community and a generation that is taking with them the end of the ancient world. They're the last people who will remember what it's like to be born on the roadside, to not have learned to read or write but to have developed extraordinary skills because of it. There's a huge cliff edge that I'm seeing, so there's a great sadness to it along with the great excitement."

That sense of urgency perhaps feeds Lee's personal intensity. Under a shock of reddish hair are two wide eyes that never rest but continually take in the world, whether it's a trailer community or a writer's name on the side of a Starbucks coffee cup. It's easy to imagine him always busy, always running through some train station, always rushing from one engagement to the next. Song collecting is only one aspect of his self-assigned job. In addition to organizing songwriting programs through the EFDSS, Lee founded and continues to oversee a foundation called the Nest Collective, which arranges concerts, festivals, and community gatherings to showcase both new and traditional folk artists.

He is, however, best known as a recording artist. While his peers are flipping through books or exploring online resources to research their tunes,

"Song collecting isn't for everyone. It's hard work. It's intense and sad and scary. It's a dangerous world you go out into."

Sam Lee

he asserts, "I do the songs that I collect myself. That's my thing. I don't go to the old books and recordings. I'm out there by myself."

Lee sets the songs he collects within ingenious arrangements that often incorporate found sounds or archival recordings, nodding to an English folk tradition but more often than not working just on its periphery. His latest album, *The Fade in Time*, released last year, incorporates Traveler melodies, intricate African polyrhythms, and shimmery drones and repetitions that call to mind avant garde composers Steve Reich and Philip Glass. "I guess what I'm trying to do is make that stuff sexy," he says. "I want to augment and fashion it in a way that people will listen to it and hear it in a new context."

Both the song collecting and the song recording are part of what Lee calls a social justice mission, and it's one that he wishes more of his contemporaries would take up. "The folk music community are an enlightened and intelligent bunch, more or less, and they'll all go, 'Yeah, yeah, yeah, we love Gypsy songs.' Which is true. But I would make the statement that they're not doing enough to honor the fact that there are still singers and songs out there. They're just quite content to do what they do. So that's a little bit of frustration there, but maybe song collecting isn't for everyone. It's hard work. It's intense and sad and scary. It's a dangerous world you go out into."

Still, he insists, "It's an amazing time for folk music in terms of there being such a diversity of stuff that's come out from the alternative side. They're putting out some interesting music – re-forming it, re-shaping it, re-fashioning the traditions."

I want to ask him to elaborate, but he is off, out of the coffee shop and into the station. Just before he disappears from sight, he is running across the concourse, his scarf trailing behind him, looking like he might actually vault over the

turnstile. In his dash, he's updating another old folk tradition: that of the itinerant train jumper.

A Second Revival

Around the time American teens were discovering the ecstasies of rock and roll and their English counterparts were starting skiffle bands, a slightly older generation of musicians was plumbing a much more local form of folk music. This was what Wall called the second folk revival. Starting in the 1950s, such artists as A.L. Lloyd and Ewan MacColl, among many others, located the spirit of England in rural pubs and urban folk clubs, where all were invited to sing because all had something to say. It was during this time that many of the ideas and conventions that still define folk music more than 50 years later emerged: communal performances, far removed from the pop circuit, with as little division as possible between artist and audience.

As a new generation began collecting, performing, and recording, the concept of folk music began to shift and expand beyond its rural and agricultural origins. Back at the Cecil Sharp House, Smyth explains: "When you look at A.L. Lloyd and Ewan MacColl, they started trying to find the folk songs of their time, which meant industrial songs. They must have been looking at those earlier collectors to see how they defined folk song, and then extrapolating it to fit their time. They started to look at coal miners and factory workers."

This is how folk music, like any art form, progresses: in a series of rebellions against the perceived purism of a previous generation. Even as some artists and song collectors argued that folk must be sung a cappella to be authentic, others developed a distinctive style of folk guitar playing, chief among them Davy Graham. His iconic 1959 composition "Angi" features a fluid melodicism and a crisp picking style, and it made the

acoustic guitar synonymous with folk music. His 1965 album with Shirley Collins, *Folk Roots New Routes*, established a duo line-up — male guitarist and female vocalist — that is still prevalent 50 years later. Graham, however, was soon overshadowed by Bert Jansch and John Renbourn, roommates who haunted the folk clubs and held impromptu six-string duels in their London apartment. Their 1966 album *Bert and John* remains foundational, and two years after its release, they formed Pentangle, the pioneering and wildly popular folk-jazz band.

The late 1960s saw an explosion in English folk music, which jibed perfectly with the hippie ideals that defined the era. Named for the dilapidated hotel where most of its members lived, Fairport Convention might have found inspiration in Bob Dylan, even covering "If You Gotta Go, Go Now" on their third album, 1969's *Unhalfbricking*, but they combined folk and rock music in a way that sounded specifically English. Only a teenager when he joined the band, Richard Thompson was already an inventive and intuitive guitar player. Sandy Denny possessed a gracefully commanding voice, which injected traditional songs as well as new compositions with a gritty sense of determinism. On 1969's *Liege & Lief*, they effectively deconstructed folk songs and turned them into rambling rock jams, transforming the 16th-century Scottish ballad "Tam Lin" into a psychedelic and proto-feminist epic.

That lineup, however, wouldn't last long; Denny left the group to pursue a solo career, while Thompson and founding member Ashley Hutchings came and went over the years. Pentangle likewise splintered, and the hippie ethos curdled into something more decadent as the '70s wore on, as England weathered a massive depression, as punk arose as a vehicle for disenfranchised youth. Artists like John Martyn and the late fiddler Dave Swarbrick continued making albums well into the '80s and '90s, although they sound somewhat out of place, coupled with the production techniques of those decades. Nick Drake, English folk music's most famous and romanticized casualty, sadly did not live to make more than three albums, but his music did enjoy a resurgence in the late 1990s thanks to a Volkswagen commercial.

One thing that connected these disparate artists working in the second half of the 20th century was their shared reliance on the Cecil Sharp House as a resource for study and inspiration. "They started to come here and started to root through those original manuscript collections, going through Folk Song Society journals, looking for music to use in their own work," says Smyth. Even today, "folksingers, if they're looking for material to sing, they don't want to sing the Fairport Convention version, because it's already so popular. People want to find that alternative version, the one people might not have heard before. You want to be able to put your own interpretation on something, so going back to some of these old versions allows for more opportunity to create your own style and put your stamp on it."

"Probably the biggest thing is putting the manuscripts of some of the leading song collectors online in the Full English Collection," Wall adds. "They've been digitized and catalogued, and they're all posted on our website, which is freely accessible."

A Strange Aura

As Lisa Knapp sings, she shields the sun from her eyes. Such a warm, cloudless day is a rarity in London, especially in late winter. The London native is sitting on the promenade in front of the Southbank Centre, a conglomerate of restaurants, theaters, and concert facilities nestled on the banks of the Thames. The London Eye towers behind us, the river sprawls before us, and

seemingly the city's entire population saunters by in the sunshine. Knapp today is among the folk, taking an impromptu floor spot in public. She is half-singing, half-reciting a verse from a traditional May song:

A man, a man whose life's a span
He flourishes like a flower
He's here today and gone tomorrow
He's vanished all in an hour

She takes a moment to consider the sentiment, briefly surveying the mass of humanity around us. "That's a bit heavy," she laughs. "It just appears in this merry little song. I find the juxtaposition of the macabre and the despicable with these very sweet melodies incredibly strange and compelling."

This is one of several May songs Knapp is currently working on for a new EP, a sequel of sorts to 2012's *Hunt the Hare — A Branch of May*. "Some folk songs are about a certain time of year rather than about a person or a story or an issue," she explains. "May has been celebrated in northern Europe for a long time. I think the earliest records go back to the 13th century, when there are records of people celebrating the end of winter and the coming of summer. It's a profound thing to celebrate. There are carols that have a strange aura about them, and they often have a verse that's telling you to make the most of your time."

It's tempting to say that Knapp is the most ambitious and modern-sounding of contemporary English folk musicians, an artist who not only has a vision for the music but also the means to make that vision a reality. A native of South London, she studied violin as a child but found the classical repertoire uninspiring. Pop music — acid house and rock and roll — held greater, albeit guiltier pleasures. She took up guitar and started jamming with her friend, the singer-songwriter Naomi Bedford. Like most teenagers, Knapp's study was self-directed. "You used to have those things called second-hand record

shops. I used to love going to those. You could find some absolute gems. You had to figure out how to find access to things you didn't really know about."

That course of study eventually brought her to Martin Carthy's "spellbinding" songs from the '60s and to his contemporary Anne Briggs, whom Knapp describes as "one of the first voices I heard that had a British accent." She started attending a local folk club in South London, where she was often the youngest person in the room and where she received an intense education in the folk songbook.

Remarkably, Knapp brings all those phases to bear in her music, which carries elements of rock, dance, balladry, singer-songwriter fare, and world music. *Wild & Undaunted* in 2008 proved a fine debut and a fitting introduction to her method of using traditional instruments in wholly new ways. But she emerged as a much more commanding presence five years later on *Hidden Seam*, an artist intent on finding a balance between the old and the new, between a song's history and its potential. A collection of songs about water — the ocean, the sea, and the men and women who make their lives on it — *Hidden Seam* sounds like nothing else coming from England's folk scene. Knapp uses these tunes as small canvases for large seascapes, incorporating otherworldly sound effects, eerie percussion, unsettling drones, and vocal acrobatics that might have more to do with avant garde singer Meredith Monk than with Sandy Denny. *Hidden Seam* is both reverent to its source material yet somehow irreverent.

"I wouldn't presume to put myself in a position where I feel I'm passing it on," Knapp says of folk music traditions. "I'm just trying to get the song to work in a way that feels right. I do enjoy looking at the history of a song, but sometimes the academic stuff can get in the way. It needs to work as a story."

And while purists may scoff at the liberties she takes, Knapp knows the songs can shoulder the weight. "That's part of their story," she says. "That's how you get so many variants of these tunes. They run off to the States, or someone makes up a new verse. It's like [a game of telephone]. That's in their heritage."

Man may vanish in an hour, in other words, but folk songs endure.

Re-Centering

Josienne Clarke lays her hands on the rough wood tabletop and makes a circle with her thumbs and index fingers. "If you imagine the folk scene as a circle," she says, "if you were talking to [famed guitar player] Martin Simpson or [Nottingham fiddler] Sam Sweeney, they'd be telling you what's inside this circle and only that." Those are the traditionalists, she explains, the artists who've been playing what is commonly considered a pure form of folk music for decades. "They all play with each other. It's a very cohesive scene, and small." With a forefinger of her right hand she points to the ridge of her left: "Sam Lee and us and Stick in the Wheel and the Unthanks and the Rheingans Sisters as well, we've all got one foot in this circle and one foot out. It's quite an interesting and useful place to make music."

Clarke is sitting in an airy coffee shop called Tintico, sipping a soy latte while her musical partner, Ben Walker, nurses an Americano across the table. The pair are here in Finchley, a sleepy commuter neighborhood in north London, to work on mixes for their new album, tentatively titled *Overnight*, at a studio nearby. Due in October, it will be their first full-length for Rough Trade, the UK record label better known for punk and post-punk acts like the Smiths, Camper Van Beethoven, the Swell Maps, and Young Marble Giants. That they might be out of place on that roster doesn't escape them; in fact, Clarke and Walker enjoy being on the periphery. "You could spend your life only playing folk in upstairs of pubs,"

says Walker. "But you'll only ever be performing traditional songs in traditional ways. If that's all you want to do, then fine. Embrace it with both hands."

He and Clarke, however, want something more. Together, they make music that is at once lush and austere, couched in history yet quietly innovative, full of subtle flourishes and unresolved drama. Clarke sings in an expressive soprano, capable of great power but usually restrained, subdued, as though keeping some essential secret from the listener. She sounds like a more ethereal Sandy Denny or a less precious Joan Baez. Her classical training, however, has led many to dismiss her. "I take issue with the idea that a trained voice can't sing folk music emotively, that you have to have some sort of rustic authenticity," she says. "I do use some of those techniques, but I think my voice is only trained up to a point where it doesn't lose my sense of self."

"There's a place for virtuosity in folk music as long as it's not singing," Walker adds, noting a double standard that has stood for decades. A veteran of trad-jazz and indie-rock bands, Walker plays guitar with impossibly nimble fingers, drawing from disparate sources (Davy Graham, Richard Thompson, Radiohead's Jonny Greenwood) as he moves fluidly between lead and accompaniment, rhythm and melody. Onstage, it's always just the two of them. In the studio, they might dress the songs up a bit, adding piano or brushed drums or possibly a saxophone solo courtesy of Clarke, but they choose and place each element with fastidious economy. Everything must complement those two crucial instruments.

In 2013 the UK folk indie label Navigator Records released the duo's debut, *Fire & Fortune*, but Clarke and Walker put out its follow-up, *Nothing Can Bring Back the Hour*, on their own label. "It's really small," Clarke says, "in that it has about two artists, and we are them." Throughout their short career, the duo

has devoted almost as much time to boxing up mail orders, designing posters and album covers, and booking tours as it has to rehearsing, performing, and recording. That's due in part to the scene being so small and resources so scarce, but it's mostly been a means to maintain strict control over their music. They did not pursue a bigger label contract and were surprised when Rough Trade pursued them.

Overnight represents a small departure for the duo, in that there are no traditional songs. Most of the tracks will be Clarke's originals, which tend to be hearty compositions that fit naturally alongside older tunes, and there will be just a handful of covers. One is a 16th-century lute ballad, another a poem adapted from the Edwardian composer Ivor Gurney. And then there is a Gillian Welch song, which is sure to inspire some discussion: Are Clarke and Walker setting their sights on America? Are they stepping outside of the circle of English folk once and for all? Or are they simply casting a wide net, finding inspiration wherever it rears its head? "When you deal with traditional music," says Clarke, "you're trying to add something of yourself from your own time, so that it carries on."

In other words, what she and Walker are doing is exactly what their contemporaries are doing — and exactly what folk musicians have done for centuries: taking meaningful material from the world around them, pushing at the boundaries of the form, and re-centering the circle for the next generation.

They are not part of a new revival, if only because folk music doesn't really move forward through revivals and resurgences. What is much more important to this music are the lulls between revivals, when the music reverts to its populist — and underground — status. Folk moves forward not at award shows or conferences, but at neighborhood pubs, coffee shops, and local events held by devoted fans. ∎

"I find the juxtaposition of the macabre and the despicable with these very sweet melodies incredibly strange and compelling."

Lisa Knapp

COLLECTIVE WISDOM

Scotland's King Creosote makes music from the far corners *by Cara Gibney*

MOBILE RECEPTION IN CRAIL, the Scottish fishing village where Kenny Anderson lives, is too patchy for a phone call. Forget Skype — the internet connection is worse. Despite his inability to rely on these modern necessities for communicating with the outside world, the proudly Scottish folksinger, who performs under the name King Creosote, remains true to the land of his birth. "Right at the beginning I was playing Scottish and Irish folk reels on the accordion," he says over the phone from his landline. "I was of the opinion that if my music was good enough, people would travel to see me."

Location is an ongoing theme in Creosote's music, attitude, and life. The windblown separation of a relatively isolated fishing village acts as emotional netting for his songs as they bite, confound, and charm. He's not out to make it easy — he crosses genres and a range of techniques and styles, from synths to traditional accordion. His earthbound falsetto is so calming it washes the intricacies of daily existence out to sea, only to bring them all back again on the flowing tide of another song.

King Creosote's career has established him as an indie-folk luminary, and over two decades it has led to the creation of iconic Fence Records and Fence Collective, and the release of over 50 albums in his own right — on Fence as well as other labels. Fence Records stopped operating in 2013, but King Creosote, steeped in the collective's do-it-yourself ethic, carries the torch with his new venture, Alter Ego Trading Company.

Beyond Accordion

Born in 1967, Creosote was a mod at heart. His earliest musical influences included English punk/mod band The Jam and the UK ska revival that gave birth to 2 Tone music. His guilty pleasures were pop groups like Adam and the Ants and Dexys Midnight Runners, and he had a soft spot for electronic artists like Depeche Mode.

His father, Billy Anderson, was playing in a successful ceilidh band — "He'd call it a Scottish dance band," Creosote says — when he taught his son how to play the accordion. Despite his early adoption of Scottish and Irish accordion songs, Creosote admits it wasn't the only kind of music he cared about when he was young, much to his father's dismay. "I was buying ['80s synth-pop band] Visage records," he recalls, "and dad was in the background moaning, 'what's this rubbish you're listening to?'"

A lifelong musician, Billy Anderson is still playing the circuit, and Creosote confesses, "I've got his voice of 20 years ago, when I'm grumbling about long drives and how heavy the equipment is becoming." In fact, Creosote remembers clearly the impact it had on him when his dad was away on tour. Now, as a father himself, he tailors his travels so the music doesn't pull him away from home for too long.

But on tour, Creosote's live performances are intimate and funny, even spellbinding. He makes a deep connection with the audience. Malcolm Middleton, formerly of indie folk-rock band Arab Strap, is among Creosote's most talented and successful peers on the UK singer-songwriter scene. Having played many times with Fence Collective artists, Middleton says of Creosote, "I've seen him live hundreds of times … [and] the thing that stands out most is his positivity and upbeat relationship with his audience. He brings joy to the stage."

This trademark, infectious stagecraft was something Creosote honed as a street performer. On leaving university, he played and busked around Europe with the bluegrass-folk outfit Skuobhie Dubh Orchestra (pronounced Scooby-Doo). Over time they morphed into Khartoum Heroes, but eventually, after the better part of a decade, they split, sending Creosote on to other places and things.

Highs and Lows

The East Neuk of Fife is a corner of coastal Scotland that encompasses a number of fishing villages, and it was here that Creosote launched Fence Records during the mid-'90s. At the same time, he adopted the pseudonym King Creosote, an alter ego that has facilitated those delicately personal elements of his songwriting. The stage name allows him to reckon with the fact that he is really "quite shy," and has been since school days. "When I see [a reporter has] written 'Kenny Anderson said,'" he explains, "I do wince a little bit because that's not the public me. The entertaining and interesting part is King Creosote. … He definitely is not the Kenny Anderson who comes home and frets about the bills."

That self-deprecating outlook helps mark a necessary delineation between Messrs. Anderson and Creosote, and allows him to protect his more private self. "I do have low spells," he says, "and sometimes I get *really* low spells."

In 1996, after the breakup of Skuobhie Dubh Orchestra, Anderson fell into a deep depression that caused him to seek medical help. In 2013, after the demise of Fence, he badly broke his ankle, and the severe depression returned. He describes it as "functioning and not functioning." When he's depressed, he explains, "My head's in a race with itself. The things that need to be done, I don't have time for. … It's that feeling of running off a cliff."

Throughout the years, Creosote's songwriting has been both the main beneficiary and the key healer of his depressions. "My biggest song counts occur in those periods coming out of depression," he says. In one year alone, he penned around 50 songs. "Within a song, you're searching for answers. In the downturns of your life, when you can't speak to people, it all goes down on the page, and you use your songs in a weird way to try and heal yourself."

The numerous albums he has released so far are a testament to this, shape-shifting as they do from heartfelt to idiosyncratic, approachable to inventive, collaborative to solo. He has released a number of records with other labels, including Domino, but says, "music on my own label is a lot more experimental.

"As a solo artist," he adds, "I'm always looking, in a way, to be led by the nose into some other sonic realm. A good song is one that, when I go back to it the next day, I think, What the hell is that? But

> ## "Within a song, you're searching for answers. In the downturns of your life, when you can't speak to people, it all goes down on the page, and you use your songs in a weird way to try and heal yourself."
>
> King Creosote

after spending some time listening to it, I get it. ... I know if that's happened to me, it'll take a bit longer for someone who didn't actually work on it [to understand it]. But it's euphoric when you do eventually get it."

Better Together

King Creosote's first album, *Queen of Brush County*, was released by Fence Records back in 1998. Fence, he says, grew into a collective of "like-minded and/or shy, and/or awkward, and/or lazy individuals who didn't want to be rock stars." The collective gathered a dazzling pool of talent from Scotland and across the border in England, including folk-rock singer-songwriter Rozi Plain, ex-punk indie-folk artist James Yorkston, and the man who ran proceedings at Fence for ten years: electro-folk singer-songwriter Johnny Lynch, who performs under the moniker of the Pictish Trail.

Through the collective, Creosote went on to become a leading light in what he calls "a sort of DIY movement." The artists that Fence supported "were only there as long as they wanted to be there," he says. "No money complications, no contract. [They] didn't sign with anybody." The collective ran its own festivals, listened to its members' ideas, burned its own CDs, and hand-stamped or -sprayed the artwork. Its approach to releasing

music was redolent of punk — something Creosote recognizes. "Punk was a reaction against the status quo," he says, "but for us it was more desperation than a reaction. [We felt like,] if we don't do this for ourselves, nobody else is going to do it."

Nowadays, Rozi Plain has three albums under her belt and plays with folk-rock outfit This Is The Kit, among others. She is well aware of the difference that the Fence Collective made for her when she joined. "They released my first album [2008's *Inside Over Here*], invited us to play at lots of shows and festivals, took us on our first tours, and have just been generally encouraging and positive about the stuff we're doing."

Singer-songwriter Dan Wilson, whose stage name is Withered Hand, is another notable Fence alumnus. He says his time with Fence and King Creosote made a massive impact on his fledgling songwriting career. "[Fence] gave me enough confidence when I had very little," he says. "[Creosote] is a great example of someone who hasn't compromised too much over the years and steered his own course. I think many respect him for that. He isn't a hype merchant. He just sticks to his guns and still believes in the power of songs."

Indeed, Creosote's songs and albums have power. The sheer number of them is too myriad to account here. When asked, he is hard-pressed to choose a favorite child. He likes *Flick the Vs,* with its mix of

gauzy gentle tones and faster-paced danceable numbers. *Diamond Mine*, his 2011 collaboration with electronica artist Jon Hopkins, brought a Mercury Prize nomination and a new audience to King Creosote's music. "*Diamond Mine* was very heart-on-sleeve and very vulnerable," he says of an album saturated with emotional detail, the electronica stepping playfully at the heels of Creosote's soulful folk. His highly acclaimed 2014 release, *From Scotland with Love*, soundtracked a film for the Glasgow Commonwealth Games. The music's emotion is stirring, the choruses rousing, and the melodies beautiful.

Creosote's push to ratify alternative, under-known talent continues. At press time, he had just finished a collective record on his Alter Ego Trading Company label, and he recently released an album titled *King Creosote & the Queens of Brush County*. Crossing genres has always been in his bones, and while his folk roots radiate from the East Neuk of Fife, his music reaches the far corners of universal emotion in its depth, versatility, and message. The well from which Creosote plumbs his songs shows no sign of running dry. His trail of albums continues to grow, while he nurtures a fundamentally DIY record label. The task of keeping it all afloat may seem daunting for the gifted, driven Scot. He, however, is unperturbed. "I don't see it as work," he says. "I see it as a privilege." ∎

Signs of the Times

RELICS OF THE '90S FROM
SONJA NELSON AND ANDY NELSON

In recent years, a flood of roots artists — the Decemberists, Fleet Foxes, the Head and the Heart, Noah Gundersen, the list goes on — has poured out of the Pacific Northwest. Some were born and raised there, and most came of age on the heels of the great do-it-yourself movement of the '90s, when homemade fliers and self-published zines were Xeroxed and screen-printed in apartments in Portland, Olympia, Seattle, and other towns inspired by these scenes.

So we turned to Andy Nelson — a former Lost Highway Records executive who was a giant fan and active member of that scene — for mementos from the era. As we leafed through his collection of these handmade relics, we unearthed considerable crossover between the punk-affiliated scenes of the 1990s and the burgeoning folk and indie roots movement. This wasn't particularly surprising. After all, one of this publication's founding editors, Grant Alden, was previously an editor at *The Rocket*, the biweekly Seattle paper that came to define grunge music.

All this crossover was a side effect of these styles and people sharing the same cities, the same clubs and venues, and the same DIY ethos. — *Kim Ruehl*

opposite:

Bikini Kill Activity Book, 1990

This activity book was a homemade zine distributed by members of Bikini Kill. As with other Bikini Kill zines (and drummer Tobi Vail's *Jigsaw*), the Activity Book includes song lyrics, essays, information about other women in music, and more. All of this is presented with riot grrrl values: feminism, anti-racism, and other socio-political concerns.

calling all grrrls and women!

the riot grrrls in and around Washington DC
are organizing a three-day riot grrrl convention
this summer. we invite
all grrrl and feminist bands
and performers, grrrl fanzine
writers, and energetic
grrrls and boys
from across the country
to contribute their skills,
energy, anger, creativity
and curiosity. we will be having
at least three shows, as well as
workshops on everything
from self-defense,
to how to run a
soundboard and
how to lay out a zine.
plus, there will be a lot of
time to talk with
other women about how
we fit (or don't fit!) in
the punk community.

RIOT GRRRL CONVENTION

July 31
August 1
August 2
Washington DC

GO!

*what bands
are playing?*

*what else
is going on?*

*where can
I stay?*

riot grrrl!
850 north edison st.
arlington, va 22205
or call
301/935-5463

Riot Grrrl Convention Flier, 1992

The DIY punk scenes of Olympia, Washington, and Washington, DC, had a lot of crossover during the '90s, as bands likeBikini Kill and Bratmobile divided their time between the two towns. This bicoastalism is part of what helped this particular DIY movement spread beyond the Northwest.

"Mary Lou Lord ... — [who] lived for a time in Olympia in the mid-1990s and recorded for that city's Kill Rock Stars label — opened the show with her new, five-piece band. The formerly girlish singer has been transformed into an engaging, mature performer."

PATRICK MacDONALD,
SEATTLE TIMES STAFF CRITIC, 1998

**Whiskeytown / Mary Lou Lord
Live at the Showbox, 1998**

This screen-printed flier from a 1998 show at Seattle's
Showbox venue presented a bill shared between
ND favorites from the Geffen label and a riot grrrl
folksinger who launched her career on Kill Rock Stars.

FRI. MARCH 3rd.

INFINITE PRODUCTIONS PRESENTS...

BIKINI KILL

PHRANC

TEAM DRESCH

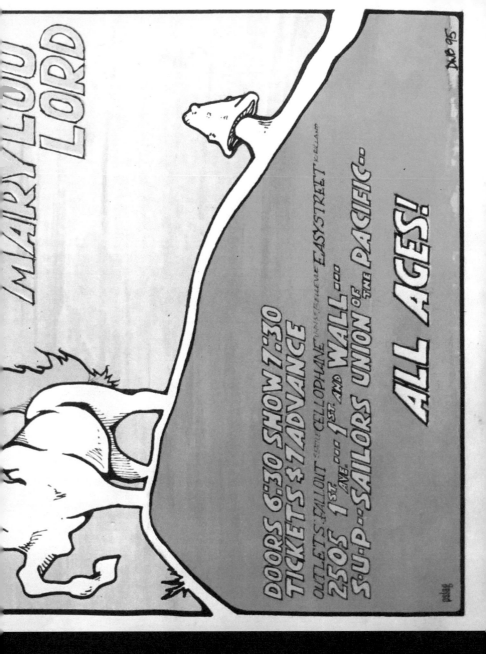

Bikini Kill / Phranc / Team Dresch / Mary Lou Lord Live at SUP Auditorium, 1995

Though Team Dresch never released an album on Kill Rock Stars, the label's compilation releases included tracks from the band, and Donna Dresch was considered a mentor by many in the Olympia music scene. KRS founder Slim Moon has credited Phranc and Mary Lou Lord with being among the first wave of acoustic players who caught his ears

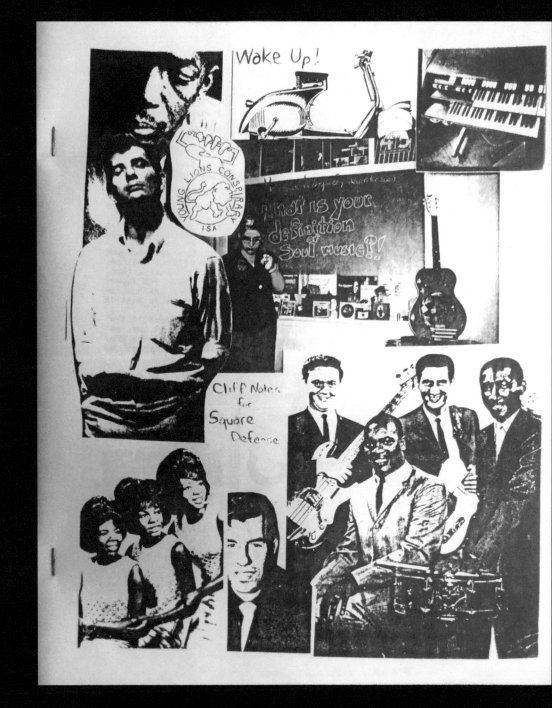

Young Lions Conspiracy Zine, year unknown

The YLC logo appeared on zines and album covers of artists in the punk/hardcore/straight-edge scene of the '90s. YLC artists were fans of everything from jazz and folk to classic R&B. One of its strongest torchbearers, Tim Kerr, who recorded for KRS and other labels, has been a Kerrville New Folk Finalist and was inducted into the Texas Music Hall of Fame in 1996.

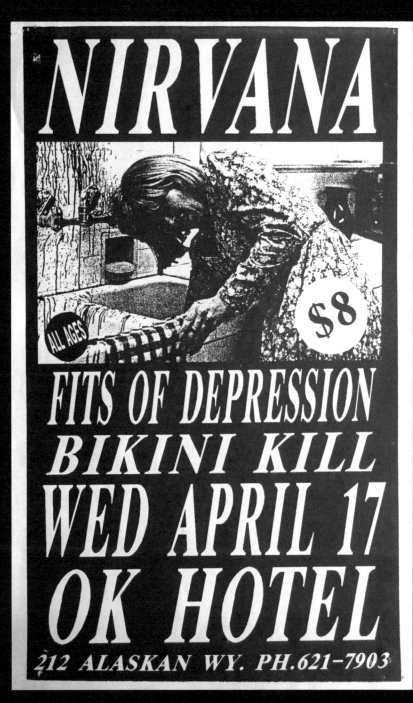

**Nirvana / Fits of Depression /
Bikini Kill Live at OK Hotel, 1991**

Though Seattle's burgeoning grunge scene was viewed by
Olympia's riot grrrl community as a different universe, many
of the players shared bills, made fliers and zines together, and
promoted each other. Nirvana was included — along with Bikini
Kill — on the first *Kill Rock Stars* compilation this same year.

PENDULUM SWINGER

**Kill Rock Stars'
quarter-century of
punks, folkies, and
intertwined roots**

by Kim Ruehl

> **"Some people would say it was more about simplicity, or it was more about feminism, or it was more about DIY and all-ages shows. [But what was happening in Olympia was] really different than what was going on in a lot of the underground scene in the rest of the country, and *really* different than what was going on in Seattle."**
>
> Slim Moon

ONE SUMMER DAY IN THE EARLY aughts, Portia Sabin and Slim Moon loaded up their car with vinyl and drove from their home in Olympia, Washington, to Portland, Oregon, for a party. "It was basically a whole bunch of small labels coming together with a crate of vinyl and selling it," Sabin remembers, "and sitting in a yard in the summertime, [at] a bar. A few people played in the upstairs room above the bar, and one of those people was Colin Meloy, who was playing a solo set."

She pauses with the excitement of the memory. "I went up to see him," she continues. "I came back down after the second song and I said, 'Slim, you've got to see this guy, he's incredible.' He didn't want to do it. He was having a conversation with someone. But I was like, 'No, get upstairs.'" Sabin knew her husband could find an audience for Meloy's band, the Decemberists. By that time, Moon had a solid track record of supporting unknown artists who were bound to blow the world's mind.

Thirteen years earlier, when he was a young punk and spoken-word artist on the Olympia scene, Moon had gathered recordings by a bunch of his friends and released a compilation titled *Kill Rock Stars*. The album featured a track from Seattle band Nirvana who, two weeks later, would be catapulted to international stardom when they released a different song to radio: "Smells Like Teen Spirit." That song had been named after some graffiti that another friend of Moon's, Olympia-based singer and poet Kathleen Hanna, had sprayed on the wall at Nirvana headquarters one night: "Kurt smells like Teen Spirit," she wrote, one-upmanship in a game of drunken insults. As luck would have it, Hanna's band Bikini Kill was also included on Moon's 1991 compilation. Despite Nirvana's soaring success shortly after the album's release, it was Bikini Kill who would more solidly define and cement Kill Rock Stars' reputation for its first dozen years as an independent label.

Hanna and Bikini Kill were a powerhouse presence on the Olympia scene. After graduating from Evergreen College — an institution that had risen out of 1960s counterculture to be a breeding ground for progressive radicals — Hanna leased a space downtown and opened an art gallery called Reko Muse. She hosted punk bands at night, after long days of counseling women who had been beaten up by the men in their lives. When Bikini Kill formed, its music was more or less what happens when one walks away from talking to battered women and steps to a microphone in front of a growling pulse of guitars and drums. It was raw and angry and powerful and defiant. It was feminist and hopeful and determined and brash. At a time when America was happy about its latest war and the Supreme Court was reconsidering a woman's right to choose, Bikini Kill and their friends — other punk bands and poets like Moon — were lashing out through their writing, their songs, and their art.

What was gestating in Olympia was a fresh protest song movement, a revitalizing of the legacy of a previous generation that decried war and applauded anyone who added their voice to the choir. While the Greenwich Village folkies gathered around a fountain in a public park with acoustic instruments, the radical progressive feminists of Olympia, Washington, in the late 1980s and early '90s gathered in people's homes and other small spaces with electric instruments and crappy old amplifiers. Where their parents' generation raised their voices in harmony, these young punks raised theirs in a roar. They were swinging on history's pendulum, as had countless Americans before them, picking up a legacy and carrying it forward. Their complaints were the same as those of the generation that preceded them, though more strongly focused on feminism. But even their modes of reaction — self-published writing, homemade recordings, house shows — were redolent of previous movements. In the 1990s, punk *was* the folk music, so it's no surprise that one of its most definitive record labels, Kill Rock Stars, has come to shape the Pacific Northwest's indie roots scene over the past quarter-century with as much gusto as it put behind defiant punks like Bikini Kill.

Girl Night

In August of 1991, Calvin Johnson of Olympia band Beat Happening, who had started a small indie label, K Records, along with his business partner Candace Pederson, decided to throw a festival. They sent out an invitation via K Records' sizable mailing list calling for independent bands to descend on Olympia for an event they were calling the International Pop Underground. For six days, those attending IPU filled Olympia's makeshift venues. Mainstage sets went down at the Capitol Theater. The theme was a burgeoning do-it-yourself movement, and it was a catalyst event for what would become a decade when indie rock, punk, and riot grrrl music prevailed in the ears of young people worldwide. Bands that played IPU included giants of the form: Fugazi, Built to Spill, Fastbacks, the Melvins, Unwound. While the Capitol Theater shows boosted the alternative/indie/DIY movement that continues to ripple out across the music world well into the 21st century, Slim Moon was particularly impressed by what happened the night before the convention even got going.

"Somebody realized they'd made an oversight," Moon remembers. "Or somebody criticized how many boy bands there were and how few women bands they were. [But] they realized how many people were going to be in town the night before [IPU], so they threw together, kind of last minute, Girl Night. The rest of the days at IPU, there were multiple venues, but the first night — the unofficial first night — it was just one show and there were all these … they were called girl bands then.

"That's the first time I saw Heavens to Betsy," he adds. "Corin [Tucker] was just — her voice, her intensity, and her lyrics — really that was the highlight of that evening for me. For a lot of people. I think seeing these two high school girls … who sometimes play drums and guitar, sometimes play bass and guitar, sometimes play drums and bass, switching out all their instruments, playing really powerful, really simple songs, it was right in the wheelhouse of what Olympia was about. Some people would say it was more about simplicity, or it was more about feminism, or it was more about DIY and all-ages shows. [But what was happening in Olympia was] really different than what was going on in in a lot of the underground scene in the rest of the country, and *really* different than what was going on in Seattle."

Indeed, Heavens to Betsy was one of those unforgettable bands — the one you accidentally saw opening for someone else and wound up wishing they were the whole show. In her 2015 memoir *Hunger Makes Me a Modern Girl*, guitarist and *Portlandia* co-creator Carrie Brownstein remembered the first time she saw Heavens to Betsy at her college in Bellingham, Washington. "The noise they made in Heavens to Betsy was vicious and strange," she writes. "It completely changed one's notion of what it meant to be powerful onstage. It was not about strength in numbers nor in size. It had nothing to do with volume. It was about surprise. It was about knowing you were going to be underestimated by everyone and then punishing them for those very thoughts."

Brownstein's description echoes Moon's, in that she saw the entire burgeoning riot grrrl and Olympia music movement encapsulated by one daring band: "When you're part of an early movement like [Tucker] was with riot grrrl," Brownstein writes, "where she had to create a space for herself and for her audience, where every show felt like a statement, where before you could play and sing you had to construct a room, one you'd be respected in, wouldn't get hurt in, a space that allowed for or even acknowledged stories that hadn't been told before, about sexual assault, sexism, homophobia, and racism, and then, musically, you have to tear that very space down — there's not a lot of room for joking around." Even listening to Heavens to Betsy now, 25 years after Tucker's first performance at IPU, the music packs a still-urgent power.

The group's raw, raucous two-person rock sound predated the White Stripes by

"We try to put out music we think is fantastic, by artists whose work is important and they have something to say. But because you can't put them in a box, it makes it more difficult as a label because … we're not sure that someone who's a Bikini Kill fan or a Sleater-Kinney fan is also going to be a Horsefeathers fan."

Portia Sabin

a half-decade, with at least as much grit and honest power. By 1994, Brownstein and Tucker would form another band, Sleater-Kinney, that would help Kill Rock Stars become one of the most critically acclaimed indie labels in the country. (Greil Marcus named Sleater-Kinney America's best rock band in 2001, and Moon rightly notes, "If you counted up all the column inches and all the five-star ratings of all the bands in the 1990s, Sleater-Kinney was the second most critically acclaimed band [of the decade], after Radiohead.")

But in '91, as he walked out of IPU, Moon recognized he had a clear mission. He'd just released the first *Kill Rock Stars* compilation, spotlighting artists who were showcasing at the convention, with an emphasis on Olympia bands. "Looking back, this is a hard tale to believe," he explains, "but I watched how hard it was for Nirvana, for the first couple years of their existence, to get any attention from any record label. And I had watched that same problem for lots of other bands that we knew in Olympia were great, but that established labels in places like Seattle always overlooked. ... So I suddenly decided, 'Well, maybe I need to be the one to step up and start putting out Olympia bands.'"

He committed to putting out the music of Olympia locals Unwound as well as his own group, Witchy Poo. "But then pretty soon after that," he remembers, "Bikini Kill called me up. They were in Washington, DC, that summer and they ... said, 'We want to put out a record but we don't trust anybody. But we decided we trust you, so you should put out our record.'" Moon flew to DC to work out the details of the deal: 50-50, with Bikini Kill retaining artistic control. From there, the Kill Rock Stars label was off and running.

"[The compilation] sold really well because Nirvana was on it," he says. "Two weeks after the *Kill Rock Stars* compilation came out, [Nirvana's] *Nevermind* came out and it was pretty

much an overnight sensation. Lots of stores picked up copies of [our] record because it had a Nirvana track on it. Lots of fans bought the record because it had a Nirvana track. And I took all the money that came in from that and put out Bikini Kill and Witchy Poo records. Then I took the money from those and put out Heavens to Betsy and Huggy Bear."

Always Something New

Two years after the *Kill Rock Stars* compilation, Moon pulled together another, titled *Stars Kill Rock*, in 1993. This time, in addition to the punk and art-rock bands that flourished in Olympia, Moon included Kurt Cobain's friend Mary Lou Lord, a folksinger and busker from Boston. He released her debut album in 1994, the same year Tucker and Brownstein formed Sleater-Kinney with Portland-based drummer Janet Weiss. Though Lord and Sleater-Kinney were decidedly different artists, both found a welcoming home at Kill Rock Stars — a fact that Moon recognizes as incongruous only in retrospect.

"I have this personality trait where I always want to try something new," he says. "When I started, I was like, 'I'm only going to do interesting guitar bands like Unwound and feminist riot grrrl bands like Bikini Kill.' We stuck to that for a little bit, until I saw Mary Lou Lord and Elliott Smith, and I was like, 'I love these solo acoustic singers. I have to do that too.'

"I had Phranc," he adds. "I put out Mary Lou Lord and Phranc. Those were different [artists from the riot grrrls] but they kind of fit because Kill Rock Stars was putting out so many woman-fronted bands at the time. ... Phranc was like a godfather of riot grrrl and Mary Lou Lord had riot grrrls in her band."

Moon's interest in Lord's music laid the groundwork in his mind for deciding it might make good sense to support Elliott Smith. After a good while of Moon

trying to find Smith another home — a label whose audience might be receptive to a solo artist whose music was as fragile as that — Moon released the singer-songwriter's eponymous debut on Kill Rock Stars in 1995.

"It barely got reviewed," Moon remembers. "It was the only record that I ever made personal calls to journalists and editors, saying, 'I know, I know, I know ... him calling himself by his own name makes it sound like he thinks he's James Taylor, but you really need to listen to this. It's really good.'"

Moon's pleas fell on deaf ears, though. Despite his support of Phranc and Lord, the media and the fans had come to expect that Kill Rock Stars released loud, raw punk rock. "[*Elliott Smith*] sold really poorly," Moon laments. "But some artists started to pick up on it. He went on tour with Mary Lou Lord and then he went on tour with John Doe, and then he went on tour with Danielle Howle. ... I think that being on Kill Rock Stars and putting his record out under his own name really hurt his discovery."

There, Moon pauses, as if to consider the late songwriter who — almost too literally — died of a broken heart; whose music was so remarkably heartfelt, it helped shift the way indie fans heard music as the 1990s drew to a close. For as popular as Smith became at the end of the decade, his rise was riddled with resistance from almost all sides — with Moon as one of the only early exceptions.

"I had several people working for me," Moon remembers, "[and my signing Elliott] horrified them. It was not a popular signing at the time. They did not get it."

He laughs, then adds: "They were all punk rockers."

Zines and Scenes

In 1988, a few years before Moon set Kill Rock Stars in motion, Olympia-based drummer Tobi Vail started self-publishing a fanzine called *Jigsaw*.

"I have this personality trait where I always want to try something new. When I started, I was like, 'I'm only going to do interesting guitar bands like Unwound and feminist riot grrrl bands like Bikini Kill.' We stuck to that for a little bit, until I saw Mary Lou Lord and Elliott Smith, and I was like, 'I love these solo acoustic singers. I have to do that too.'"

Slim Moon

Along with a handful of other similar publications, *Jigsaw* was one of the defining forces in what became Olympia's riot grrrl community. (Vail coined the movement's spelling.) It shared poems and rants about politics, feminism, and music, and the places where all three intersect. It was in *Jigsaw* that Vail announced the birth of her almost-all-grrrl band Bikini Kill, which she'd started with local poet/women's counselor Kathleen Hanna.

Hanna and others were frequent contributors to *Jigsaw*, always sticking to the political and feminist angle of the zine. The efforts of these young punks and poets were singular in history: young women taking control of their own community through music, performance, and political discourse.

Three years into its existence, in 1991, *Jigsaw* announced the formation of a Eugene, Oregon-based punk duo called Bratmobile, whose co-founder Molly Neuman, a Washington, DC, native, published her own zine, *Girl Germs*. Bratmobile had formed when Neuman and Allison Wolfe met at the University of Oregon, gravitating around one another like a pair of planets in a universe full of space trash. They were punks in a sea of hippies, and they started hitching rides to Olympia on the weekends to hang

out with what they quickly realized was "their crowd."

The duo was younger than a lot of the other bands in the scene, and their songs a little less confrontational. Where they tackled abusive men and the war in Iraq, it was through ridicule and mockery instead of the hard hammer wielded by Hanna and others. They excoriated the popular girls with songs like "Cool Schmool" ("You're so cool yeah yeah / fuck you too! Cool schmool!") and unpacked culturally internalized gender dynamics with simple tunes like the incredibly infectious "Girl Germs" ("Girls are the rots you insist / by pulling my ponytail you persist").

They hit the road, landing in Neuman's hometown (and Hanna's). What they found in the nation's capital was a parallel community of young feminist, anti-war musicians who were making similar music. It wasn't long before Bratmobile franchised itself, starting a group called Bratmobile DC and chronicling the Bratmobile efforts on both coasts in the pages of their zine named for one of their catchiest tunes.

And right about here is where our story starts to sound perhaps too biblical, with this person begetting that, and so on and so forth. Indeed, following the threads of Olympia's punk and riot grrrl

scenes toward the indie roots community that prevails across the Pacific Northwest now, 25 years into Kill Rock Stars' tenure, one starts to realize it's more of an intricately woven web than it is a straight line. One must remember that Kurt Cobain was a Lead Belly fan, that singer-songwriter Jeremy Enigk (of Sunny Day Real Estate) taught Brownstein to play the guitar, that Kathleen Hanna — and Slim Moon — began as poets and spoken-word artists. This community that had formed around common political opinions spoke out about these concerns with poems and songs, DIY publications and house parties; gave rise to loud, unbridled, unselfconscious punk; and rode its spinning top through a decade of speed and wobbles, moving in spirals across the green, lush Northwest ground. As it happened, when that top settled, as a new century loomed, it landed on either side of Olympia — in Portland and Seattle — pointing, somehow, toward quieter instrumentation and deeply rooted acoustic music.

Not for nothing, the passion and exacting musicianship of Olympia's punk and riot grrrl scenes — and Seattle's grunge explosion — turned high school and college students across the country on to the idea that musicians need not wait to be discovered by major

Slim Moon at the punk house called the
Alamo — Olympia, Washington, 1986.

Colin Meloy (The Decemberists) began
his career as one of Portia Sabin and
Slim Moon's great discoveries.

record labels. Before the internet was even as basic as a series of chat rooms, there were mail-order zines like *Jigsaw* and pen pals and the bootlegging of cassette compilations.

It was the latter that landed a copy of *Stars Kill Rock* in my 16-year-old hands, thousands of miles away from Olympia, Washington, in Florida. I had a teenage lifetime of music study and books full of original poetry. I was popular-ish at school but upset about the world. A compilation made by people ten years my senior was a lifeline at the time, a peephole to the other side of a door, where there were others who thought as I did, who saw music as an avenue for liberation and courageous honesty. I devoured the compilations and albums released by the bands on them: Team Dresch, Bikini Kill, Heavens to Betsy, Bratmobile. I eventually found my way to Portland and then Seattle, pulled almost unconsciously by the daring of the music.

I wasn't alone, by a long shot. Around the same time, in a Minnesota dorm room, a young punk songwriter named Laura Veirs started hearing echoes of a feminist punk scene in the Pacific Northwest. The Colorado native was a workhorse of a songwriter, and it took no time for her to find a mirror in the Olympia grrrl bands and feminist politicism of other groups from that region.

After college, Veirs moved briefly to Seattle in 1997 — the same year Sleater-Kinney released their groundbreaking *Dig Me Out* record and Elliott Smith finally caught a break with *Either/Or*.

"I found out about the indie rock and grrrl scene through the underground college network," Veirs recalls. "It was a huge revelation [for me] that there was this longstanding feminist music scene that I could get involved in if I lived there. My brother was living in Seattle, and that's why I moved there … when I graduated college. I thought I was going to continue this punk band that I had started — this all-girl punk band — but that broke up, so I just struck out on my

Elliott Smith performing for the *XO* release party, at Tower Records on Mercer Street in Seattle, 1998.

own and joined other bands, and really started my solo thing at that point. That's where [my idea] of 'I can do this as a punk performer' [started]. But I was playing acoustic instruments, so I was making that shift around that time too, and discovering old country music, old folk music, even while I was a punk. I was like, 'Wait, there's this other thing — Gillian Welch and Mississippi John Hurt.'"

Veirs, whose critically acclaimed solo recordings include intricate indie roots music as well as traditional folk ballads, drifted for a while, but eventually found her tribe in Portland. By that time, riot grrrl was the prevailing culture. It had outgrown its home in the underground, leaving somewhat of a

chasm in the Northwest's predilection for counterculture. There, artists like Veirs, who'd gravitated to Portland and Seattle in search of their punk peers, discovered something that was, perhaps, more punk than punk rock. They started forming large orchestral folk groups and tight, gritty old-time bands.

Veirs met and started working with a young record producer named Tucker Martine, now her husband, who had also landed in Portland after a spell in Seattle.

Martine, who has worked on some of the most stunning indie roots recordings of the past 20 years — the Decemberists' *The Crane Wife*, Aoife O'Donovan's *Fossils*, Langhorne Slim's *Be Set Free*, Abigail Washburn's *City of Refuge*, and

"If you counted up all the column inches and all the five-star ratings of all the bands in the 1990s, Sleater-Kinney was the second most critically acclaimed band [of the decade], after Radiohead."

Slim Moon

Veirs' entire catalog — has witnessed the evolution of Northwest music from punk to roots, from a slightly different perspective.

"Things like banjos and fiddles," he says, "have been around long before there was riot grrrl or grunge. ... [Besides,] Elliott Smith fronted a hard-rocking band before you ever heard his song-writery stuff. Steve Turner was writing folk songs on his off-time from [Mudhoney].

"No music comes from nothing," he asserts. "It's all an amalgamation of various things that came before it, so I tend to see plenty of things in common between seemingly disparate artists. Portland has, until recently, been relatively inexpensive to live in and hasn't had much in the way of music industry presence, so that makes everything that [has happened] here underground."

What was happening underground in the early 2000s was that artists like the Decemberists' Meloy and Veirs, and orchestral folk outfit Horsefeathers (another KRS artist), were swirling around the open mics, house shows, and acoustic nights at bars like the Laurelthirst Pub. They drove up to Seattle and played the Crocodile, which is where Veirs ran into Slim Moon one night when she was opening for her buddies in the Decemberists.

"I was over the moon," she says, groaning at her own intentional pun. "He was just so cool. But I had heard about him for years, he was just such a legend. We struck up a friendship and ... I don't remember how it happened, but he [became] my manager."

Moon remembers more clearly the lesson he'd learned from the early days with Elliott Smith. He didn't want to do a disservice to Veirs' music by signing her to KRS when he knew from experience that the fans and media weren't quite as receptive to his singer-songwriter artists.

"I told Laura, I said, 'I think you should go more grown-up,' so I listed more grown-up labels, including Nonesuch. She wound up on Nonesuch — they loved the record. I ended up being her manager when she was ready to put out the next record on Nonesuch. Then, because I had a relationship with Nonesuch, they decided they wanted to hire a new A&R guy and they asked me if I knew anybody. I ended up calling them back and saying I would like to apply for the job.

"We helped Elliott Smith get pretty successful and then he left for [Dreamworks]," he explains. "We had helped Decemberists get pretty successful and they left for Capitol. We had helped Sleater-Kinney get pretty successful and they had left for SubPop. ... Most labels, when they get to that point, they end up selling their business to get an upstream deal with a major ... to try to create a system where a band could be successful [and stay] on that label, instead of having to move to a [different] label. But because of the manifesto of Kill Rock Stars from day one, it would have been a total betrayal of the bands who had stayed with me if I had then moved the record label to having a relationship with a major label. Bikini Kill had been very clear that they stayed with me because

I wasn't going to be that guy. But I still had this idea that I had the ear and talent to discover somebody.

"When I signed Elliott and when I signed the Decemberists," he continues, "there really wasn't any other labels trying to sign them. I was never good at winning a bidding war. What I was good at was occasionally finding an artist and taking care of them before the other labels had all figured out how talented the person was. ... So I thought if [my wife] Portia took over the label, I [could go] to Nonesuch and find a band like the Decemberists and make them as big as the Decemberists, except I'll be working with them when they're that big instead of losing them to somebody else."

Though Moon's tenure at Nonesuch was short — budget cuts targeted the newest recruits — he was grateful for the move. He landed at Ryko as an A&R guy for a while, until he did the math and realized he was working for a major with the same budget he'd had at Kill Rock Stars. Before long, he made the hard choice to walk away from the music industry entirely. Following that same tack of always wanting to try something new, these days Moon is pursuing a path as a Unitarian minister. It's a far cry from the punk clubs of Olympia, but Sabin has been carrying the KRS torch swimmingly for the past decade or so. The handoff of an influential label from husband to wife is atypical in the music business, but, given KRS's feminist history and Sabin's unique vision, it makes perfect sense.

"I think it's the coolest thing ever that he handed the label over to his wife and

Corin Tucker performs during Sleater-Kinney's 2015 reunion tour.

she continued to run it successfully," says Veirs, who now runs her own label and whose latest project, this year's *case/ lang/veirs*, produced by Martine, has her teaming up with now-Portlander k.d. lang and former Seattleite Neko Case.

"[Slim] was like 'I'm out.' And she was like, 'I'm in.' That's just so weird and cool," Veirs adds, "that it could happen and the label could continue to do well. It's a hard thing to do, to make money as a record label these days."

That is a fact that Sabin knows well, not that she's at all deterred. Few independent labels can boast a history that goes as deep and is as inextricably tied to its community — the philosophical one as well as the regional one — as is Kill Rock Stars. Twenty-five years into the label's tenure, Sabin, an anthro-

pologist in her previous life, knows well that history's pendulum keeps swinging. You just have to be ready when it shifts direction.

"If I was smart," Sabin says, "I would have a genre label. I would just have metal bands ... because those labels do fantastically well. They know their audience really well. They know their audience buys stuff. They can market to them in a really efficient way. That's a real boost for a label to have that ability. My challenge is a little bit tougher. We try to put out music we think is fantastic, by artists whose work is important and they have something to say. But because you can't put them in a box, it makes it more difficult as a label because we have to say, well, we're not sure that someone who's a Bikini Kill fan or a

Sleater-Kinney fan is also going to be a Horsefeathers fan. That's not necessarily the same group of people. So we just have to hope that people like my taste and people appreciate what we've done in the past and want to get involved with what we're thinking is great for the future.

"That said, we have a new band this year called Summer Cannibals — a Portland band who are just a fantastic rock band. ... I love the music. I think they've got a fantastic live show, a great work ethic. They have their own record label and they put out their own first two records. But also it's a little bit of a throwback. It feels like a Sleater-Kinney kind of thing," she says with a smile in her voice. "And I think our audience might resonate with that." ∎

Contributors

ALLISON MOORER is a music industry veteran who has been nominated for Academy, Grammy, Americana Music Association, and Academy of Country Music awards. Her writing has appeared in *Guernica, Performing Songwriter*, and elsewhere. She is an MFA candidate in nonfiction at the New School in New York City, where she lives with her son.

ANNE MARGARET DANIEL teaches literature at the New School in New York City. Her writing about Oscar Wilde's trials, Bob Dylan, and contemporary music has been widely published. She is currently finishing a book about F. Scott Fitzgerald. She lives in Manhattan and upstate New York with her husband.

ARIANA DIXON is a paper collage artist who draws her audience's attention with her surreal creations. She lives in Asheville, North Carolina.

CARA GIBNEY writes about music for *No Depression, fRoots*, Americana UK, *CultureHub* magazine, Gigging NI, and elsewhere. She lives in Belfast, Ireland.

CAROLYN McCOY is a writer and photographer living in Marin County, California.

CHRIS WADSWORTH is a lifelong musician, founder of the FreshGrass Foundation, and publisher of *No Depression*. He lives in San Francisco with his kids and spends as much time as he can in Montana.

COLIN SUTHERLAND is an illustrator and designer living in the mountains of North Carolina. He finds inspiration in century-old fiddle tunes, vintage print ephemera, and the bawl of his bluetick coonhound.

DEBORAH CROOKS is an Alameda, California-based freelance writer and performing songwriter. Her work has appeared in *Northern Lights, Yoga Journal*, and elsewhere.

DREW CHRISTIE is a Seattle-based animator and illustrator. His work has been featured by *The New York Times, Huffington Post, The Atlantic*, and others.

GWENDOLYN ELLIOTT is a freelance writer and former music editor of *Seattle Weekly*. She lives in the Emerald City with her husband, pets, and a lot of vinyl records.

HOWARD RAINS is an artist and fiddler obsessed with painting and playing an archaic style of fiddling from his home state of Texas. He enjoys traveling and performing with his wife and musical partner.

JENNY RITTER is a West Coast Canadian indie-folk musician/rock choir director who loves doing illustration on the side.

JONATHAN BERNSTEIN is a writer and fact-checker living in Brooklyn. His work has been published in *Oxford American, The Guardian, Rolling Stone, Pitchfork*, and *American Songwriter*.

KENT GUSTAVSON, Ph.D., is the author of the award-winning biography of Doc Watson, *Blind But Now I See* (Sumach-Red Books, 2012). He currently lives in Bonn, Germany, with his wife, pets, and guitar.

KIM RUEHL spent her 20s chasing the songwriter dream before falling into a career as a writer. She is the editor of *No Depression*, and her work has appeared in *CityArts, Seattle Weekly, Billboard*, NPR, and elsewhere. She lives in Asheville, North Carolina, with her wife and kid.

LEE ZIMMERMAN has been a freelance writer for publications like *American Songwriter, Blurt*, and *Billboard* for 20 years. He lives in Maryville, Tennessee, with his wife.

LEIGH GIBSON is a member of The Gibson Brothers, an award-winning duo from Northern New York. In 2015, he received an honorary doctorate from the State University of New York for his contribution to music.

MATT POWELL is a writer and musician from Los Angeles. He plays guitar in the Incredible Heavies, and learned many of life's lessons managing the Ernest Tubb Record Shop on Nashville's Lower Broad.

MEGAN ROMER moved from Upstate New York to South Louisiana over a decade ago, and has been writing professionally ever since. Her writing focuses on the hyper-local cultural abundance she finds every time she steps out the door.

PAUL LA RAIA has been a music photographer for over 20 years. His work appears in *Modern Drummer* and *Living Blues* magazines and he is the author of *The Levon Helm Midnight Ramble Book*.

STACY CHANDLER is the copy editor and social media manager for *No Depression*. She is a freelance journalist living in Raleigh, North Carolina, with her husband, their daughter, a big dumb yellow dog, and an underused fiddle.

STEPHEN DEUSNER is a Tennessee native now living in Bloomington, Indiana. His work appears regularly in *Pitchfork, American Songwriter, Uncut*, the Bluegrass Situation, Stereogum, Salon, and elsewhere.

Screen Door

GROWING FRESHGRASS

BY CHRIS WADSWORTH

In the past, this back-of-the-book space has been used to provide our readers with a parting thought via a closing essay. But going forward, we plan to expand the Screen Door into a separate section that we'll use to report on our progress with the Freshgrass Foundation — the nonprofit that, among other things I'll get to in a moment, owns and publishes *No Depression*.

Beginning with our next issue — coming this autumn — you'll find here a quarterly report on the foundation's activities, directly from me. I intend to be very transparent about our activities as well as our successes and failures. After all, this is a community effort. But I didn't want to just dive into these quarterly reports without first telling you what the foundation is all about.

In addition to publishing *No Depression* online and in print, the FreshGrass Foundation produces the FreshGrass Festival at Mass MoCA in North Adams, Massachusetts, every September. Our lineup this year includes Old Crow Medicine Show, Glen Hansard, Rosanne Cash, and many more. (Find the full lineup at freshgrass.com.) The foundation also conducts a number of giving programs:

The FreshGrass Commission is our annual flagship grant. Each year, we offer a one-time gift to allow an individual or band to create roughly an album's worth of original music. The music created will vary greatly in style, depending on each recipient, but we ask that every artist who receives the commission pushes the boundaries of their respective medium. The artists chosen own the music they create through the commission, but we assist in the process by giving them the time and resources to write it. The finished work will be unveiled and premiered each year at a FreshGrass event. Our inaugural recipient will be announced this summer.

The FreshGrass Award celebrates and rewards innovative artists who offer a fresh take on the tradition of bluegrass music. With four categories (band, duo, banjo, and fiddle) and prizes totaling more than $25,000, we're proud to say that our award is the most ambitious of its kind in bluegrass music today. It is one of the premier opportunities for bluegrass bands that are just setting out for a life in music. In addition to the cash award, five finalists in each category are invited to the FreshGrass Festival each year to show their stuff in front of a large audience.

FreshScores is an annual series of original scores composed by contemporary artists and performed live to classic and significant silent films. Each year we select a handful of innovative artists to offer their musical interpretation to a film of their choice. Performances take place at the FreshGrass Festival (and possibly additional locations in the near future). Our inaugural FreshScores were presented in 2015, with scores written and performed live by Alison Brown, Mamie Minch, and the Lost Bayou Ramblers. In 2016, we have scores in the works by Aoife O'Donovan, Darol Anger, and Stephane Wrembel.

The *No Depression* Writing Fellowship awards monetary assistance to writers for deep investigative reporting and storytelling related to American roots music. Fellowship stories should be 7,000-10,000 words and follow a specific theme. They will be published in the ND print journal during the following year. Applicants will need to submit a synopsis of their idea, author bio, and writing samples during open application periods. The first will be this August 15 – September 15.

FreshGrass Presents supports local bluegrass scenes by sponsoring monthly jams and special events. We believe support at such a grassroots level will strengthen the local musical ecosystem and foster the development of new bands, original music, and memorable gatherings. So far, we are supporting the Happy Dog monthly jam at the Euclid Tavern in Cleveland, Ohio, and Michael Daves' First Monday Jam at Rockwood Music Hall in New York City.

Matching grants to carefully chosen crowdfunding campaigns are aimed at helping artists' fanbases to boost creative projects. We believe crowdfunding is the best model for matching grants, since it's an avenue that allows the artist to ask fans to directly support the creative process. It also cultivates a healthy economy around the music, which is necessary in order for roots music to continue to thrive. We are proud to announce our support of the legendary Bobby Osborne's latest project as our inaugural matching grant.

So, as you can see, we have some big plans and appreciate your support — after all, your purchase of this journal has helped to fund our giving programs. We are always looking for new ideas and more creative ways to support roots music, so please don't hesitate to let us know if you have ideas to share or want to get involved in any way. See you in the fall!